THE ABC's OF THE ECONOMIC CRISIS

THE ABC's OF THE ECONOMIC CRISIS

What Working People Need to Know

Fred Magdoff
Michael D. Yates

THE ABC'S OF THE ECONOMIC CRISIS
Fred Magdoff and Michael D. Yates

Published in agreement with Monthly Review Press, New York for publication and sale only in the Indian Subcontinent (India, Pakistan, Bangladesh, Nepal, Maldives, Bhutan & Sri Lanka)

First Published in India, 2010

ISBN 978-93-5002-061-6 (Hb)

Published by
AAKAR BOOKS
28 E Pocket IV, Mayur Vihar Phase I, Delhi 110 091
Phone : 011 2279 5505 Telefax : 011 2279 5641
aakarbooks@gmail.com; www.aakarbooks.com

Printed at
Mudrak, 30 A, Patparganj, Delhi 110 091

To all those who struggle for a better world

Acknowledgments

First, we want to thank our colleagues at *Monthly Review*—John Bellamy Foster, John Simon, John Mage, Brett Clark, Claude Misukiewicz, Martin Paddio, and Scott Borchert—for their encouragement and support. We also are grateful to Carol Lambiase and Stephanie Luce, who read the entire manuscript and made many helpful comments and suggestions, as did Jan Schultz, who read an early version of the manuscript. Thanks as well to Erin Clermont for her excellent copyediting.

Contents

Preface

This short book aims to describe and explain the "The Great Recession," the most severe economic crisis since the Great Depression, in straightforward and easy to understand language. We have written it for workers, students, and activists who are trying to grasp what is happening and who want to organize and do something about it. We hope that readers will pass this book on and use our analysis to spread the word that this is no ordinary recession but a potentially deep and long-lasting downturn that could change our lives and those of our children. If we understand its magnitude and causes, we can position ourselves—politically and ideologically—to begin building a better world.

Most of the book discusses events in the United States. This is both because this is where we live and that the United States is far and away the most powerful and important capitalist country. The crisis began here and then spread to the rest of the world, a reflection of the fact that U.S. economic, political, and military power have allowed economic elites here to penetrate the economies of every part of the globe. What this means is that activists everywhere not only need to fight to reconstruct their own societies but also struggle to liberate them from the onerous burden of U.S. corporate interests. Those of us in the United States have the same duty, made more urgent by the horrors that our nation has rained down upon the rest of the world, not just the murderous bombs of war but the more mundane but no less deadly bombs of the economic policies promoted by the United States and eagerly embraced by those with power in so many countries.

If you live outside the United States, this book will still be useful to you. What has happened here has happened everywhere. The specifics differ somewhat, but the fundamental truths are the same. The economic system in which almost all of us are enmeshed is profoundly anti-human and irrational. Although a significant portion of the world's population—perhaps 20 to 30 percent—lives at a very high standard of living, even for them it is a dead-end system, hell-bent on trivializing our lives and destroying the planet, while producing misery for a huge number of people. We suffer its continuance at our peril.

WITCH 2: Fillet of a fenny snake,
In the cauldron boil and bake;
Eye of newt, and toe of frog,
Wool of bat, and tongue of dog,
Adder's fork, and blind-worm's sting,
Lizard's leg, and owlet's wing,
For a charm of powerful trouble,
Like a hell-broth boil and bubble.

ALL: Double, double toil and trouble;
Fire burn, and cauldron bubble.

—SHAKESPEARE, *Macbeth*

1. The Calm before the Storm

The economic outlook continues to be favorable.
—HENRY PAULSON, 2005

Just three years ago, in the spring of 2006, things appeared very promising. The home construction industry boomed, absorbing those looking for work and those waiting for jobs to open up and pushing down the rate of unemployment. For all of 2006, the official unemployment rate was 4.7 percent, and in the spring of that year it was about 4.4 percent. Both numbers were low by U.S. standards. Wages were rising. The Bush administration saw the numbers as justifying its economic polices: "Today's strong report shows that our economy continues to produce steady, sustainable employment growth with strong wage gains for America's workers. Average hourly earnings for workers jumped 4.2 percent in 2006, the best 12-month showing since 2000," U.S. Secretary of Labor Elaine L. Chao said in a public statement on January 5, 2007. "This is further evidence that the president's economic policies are working and producing strong wage gains for America's workers, and we should be cautious of future policies that would slow these gains."[1] Some of the money from the real estate explosion found its way into the stock market, and the most famous stock index, the Dow Jones, hit an all-time high in October 2007.

It should be expected that the president and his staff would take good economic numbers at face value and milk them for political advantage. But economists and financial experts were no different. With few exceptions, they saw a bright future. There might be some bumps in the road, but severe downturns were things of the past, of only historical interest. They believed that money managers in the world's financial centers had harnessed the techniques of advanced mathematics and statistics and learned how to handle risk. Financial markets, so they told us, acted as stabilizers, preventing too much euphoria on the upside and too much pessimism on the downside. If an unexpected sequence of events occurred that threatened prosperity, the Federal Reserve could put things right by loosening or tightening the credit strings. "Trust in the markets," said the economists and financiers. And the Fed will take care of any market instabilities before they become crises. Pick an economist or financial wizard. Maybe Alan Greenspan, chairman of the Fed, who was worshipfully proclaimed to be both "oracle" and "maestro" of the economy. Perhaps Robert Rubin, President Clinton's Secretary of the Treasury and wise man of Wall Street. Or Lawrence Summers, world-famous economist, another Clinton Treasury secretary, president of Harvard, and former chief economist at the World Bank. Were any of these luminaries warning us that—as we all now know and as left-wing economists writing in the pages of journals far removed from the mainstream, like ***Monthly Review***, were telling us for many years—that the floorboards of the economy were rotten? That housing prices could not continue to rise at a rate far surpassing the growth of the Gross Domestic Product (GDP)? That it was not possible for Wall Street to post outlandish returns year in and year out? That increasing levels of consumer, corporate, and government debt—relative to the underlying economy—couldn't go on forever? That the unimaginable growth of speculation, using ever more complex and risky ways to gamble, was inherently destabilizing? That an eternally expanding economy was as much a myth as the fountain of youth? Perhaps the most remarkable thing is that the housing bubble began almost immediately after the dot-com bubble burst. Yet few seemed to wonder how it could be that the new bubble wouldn't also burst, sooner or later.

Now, a few years later, we are living in desperate times. Every day, thousands of workers lose their jobs. In June 2009, the United States official unemployment rate hit 9.5 percent, and it will get higher in the months to come.[2] Housing prices are in free fall, and tens of millions of households are choking on debt. The titans of Wall Street have gone bankrupt or to Washington to beg for money. Colossal financial frauds have come to light, in which psychopaths like Bernard Madoff stole billions of dollars from gullible clients who thought it was their right to make high rates of returns on their money. On Main Street, tales of woe abound. A woman over ninety years old was duped by a bank into taking out a large mortgage she couldn't possibly afford. Now she may soon be homeless, as will many other poor people, often minorities, who were swindled by unscrupulous lenders. Many home buyers may have made reckless decisions. They did not cause the crisis, however. As we will show, it was the often fraudulent actions of the banks and the big Wall Street firms that created the financial mess in which we now find ourselves.

Fourteen million, seven hundred thousand people were officially unemployed in June 2009, and this does not include the nine million working part-time involuntarily (because their work hours were cut or part-time employment was all they could find) and the 2.2 million people "marginally attached" to the labor force (they were not officially unemployed but wanted a job and had searched for one in the past year; of these, there were 793,000 "discouraged workers," who had stopped looking for work because they believed no jobs were available). Adding these to the officially out of work raises the unemployment rate to 16.5 percent. Very troubling is that long-term unemployment (those out of work for at least fifteen weeks) is now at its highest level since the government began measuring it in 1948.[3] States are running out of money for unemployment compensation. In January 2009, 50,000 New Yorkers were scheduled to exhaust their unemployment benefits after receiving them for eleven months. A *New York Times* reporter tells of "Julio Ponce, a 55-year-old chef,

[who] has been using his weekly unemployment check to pay the rent on his apartment in the Bushwick section of Brooklyn since he lost his job at a center for the elderly more than a year ago. But he said he did not know how he would cover the $800 monthly rent after his unemployment benefits lapsed this week. 'No one is helping me,' said Mr. Ponce, who was faxing his résumé to hotels and restaurants from an employment office in Downtown Brooklyn on Thursday. 'I've applied for public assistance, but I don't think I'm going to get it.' "[4] Nationwide, by March of 2009, about one-quarter of the unemployed had been out of work for at least six months and many were running out of unemployment benefits, having gone through the twenty-six weeks their states provide and more than thirty weeks of extended benefits mandated by the federal government. One economist estimated that in the second half of the year, 700,000 people would exhaust their benefits.[5]

Making matters worse, our nation's unemployment compensation system is much less generous than it used to be. A lower percentage of workers receive unemployment insurance payments—only 37 percent are eligible, compared to the 50 percent during the recession in the mid-1970s. The maximum amount of time that people can receive unemployment payments has been reduced from sixty-five weeks to a standard of twenty-six weeks today, recently extended by Congress for an extra thirteen weeks (and still further in the stimulus package enacted by Congress in February of 2009). Furthermore, employers have become more aggressive in challenging unemployment claims, and many employees have discovered that they cannot collect the benefits to which they thought they were entitled. To stave off hunger, record numbers of people are seeking food stamps. At the beginning of April 2009, a record 32.2 million persons were receiving food stamp assistance, one in every ten Americans.[6] In past downturns they would have sought public assistance as well. In the 1970s, over 80 percent of the poor were eligible to receive public assistance through welfare programs such as Aid to Families with Dependent Children. Now, after the welfare "reforms" of the Clinton era, only 40 percent of the poor are eligible to receive assistance.[7]

Beneath the harsh statistics, diligent journalists, social workers, police, and mental health counselors are witnessing more ominous responses to the crisis. Increases in murders of coworkers and family members, suicides, thefts, bank robberies, arson, domestic disturbances, depression—all have been linked to the growing hard economic times in towns and cities in every part of the country. The *New York Times* reports that anxiety and depression, triggered by the economic downturn, are on the rise, with more people seeking treatment from mental health professionals. In a *Times*/CBS poll, 70 percent of respondents were worried that a household member would be jobless. And as people become desperate after losing their jobs, robberies have become more common. There have even been a rash of thefts in California of the furnishings that companies place in houses to make them easier to sell, and sometimes even plumbing and other fixtures are for sale on the black market.[8]

There is no doubt that we are in the most severe economic crisis since the Great Depression. In 1982, when we were in a deep recession, unemployment was higher than it is now. But then the Federal Reserve (the government agency that tries to influence economic activity by making credit easier or more difficult to obtain) forced interest rates on loans to record-high levels in an effort to eliminate inflation and scare the daylights out of working men and women. High interest rates were also bad for companies who needed to borrow money, and they responded in 1982 with mass layoffs, further reducing demand and also making it less likely that workers would insist on higher wages in the near future. Once inflation was tamed, the Federal Reserve pushed interest rates down and the federal government pumped money into the economy through its own spending. Within a couple of years, the economy began to recover. Today, however, the Federal Reserve has managed to get interest rates as low as it can (some rates are near zero) yet still economic activity continues to decline and will probably stabilize at a low level. We have to go back to the 1930s for a precedent, or to Japan in the 1990s—when no amount of government intervention could get the economy rolling. Already our government has spent hundreds of billions of dollars and committed trillions more to trying to get banks to open their lending windows and consumers and businesses to start borrowing, but credit is still nearly frozen and spenders are retrenching. Mortgage rates are near record lows and gasoline prices have dropped dramatically, yet houses are not selling well and car sales have tanked to the point that even the world's premier auto company, Toyota, is losing gobs of money and the weaker ones are essentially bankrupt—subsisting on government handouts. Nothing seems to be working.

What in the world has happened? We will explain in some detail what happened and why it happened. But for now, let's just take the example of the housing market, mentioned above. It's true that housing prices were at record highs and seemed like they would continue to increase. But the explosion in home building and the dramatic increase in home prices was partially a result of speculative buying: people kept purchasing houses because they thought prices would always rise. And as they kept buying, prices *did* continue to rise. It was like a Ponzi scheme in which someone promises large returns and pays these out to the first "investors" with the money hustled from later ones. Some house buyers, especially those involved early in the price escalation, cashed out and made a lot of money.

Every night on television you could tune in to a show in which savvy individuals bought houses, either fixed them up with minimal investment or not, and then "flipped" them for a much higher price. It looked like anyone willing to put in a small effort could get rich in real estate. In hot markets like Las Vegas, Southern California, and parts of Florida, home owners saw their houses double or even triple in price in a year or so. Condominiums sold two and three times before anyone moved into them. One of us was in Key West, Florida, in 2005 and saw shacks selling for a million dollars. And as house prices skyrocketed, their owners borrowed money against the appreciated value and used the money to buy more property, make additional home improvements, or purchase all manner of goods and services—helping to keep the economy going by using their homes as ATM machines.

But as we will see, the housing and mortgage market was truly a house of cards, built on low interest rates, easy money, the pushing of purchases on people who couldn't afford them, speculative fever, and the use of fraudulent tactics and misleading mortgage terms. And once a significant number of people were unable to make their mortgage payments, it became clear there was a problem. Homes offered for sale started to swamp purchases and prices fell. The falling prices forced the more indebted home owners and some speculators to sell, pushing prices down further. The bubble burst. And this was only one of the many symptoms that a major crisis that was brewing.

> The crisis was caused by the largest leveraged asset bubble and credit bubble in the history of humanity, where excessive leveraging and bubbles were not limited to housing in the United States but also to housing in many other countries and excessive borrowing by financial institutions and some segments of the corporate sector and of the public sector in many and different economies: a housing bubble, a mortgage bubble, an equity bubble, a bond bubble, a credit bubble, a commodity bubble, a private equity bubble, a hedge funds bubble are all now bursting at once in the biggest real sector and financial sector deleveraging since the Great Depression.
>
> —*RGE Monitor Newsletter*, Oct. 10, 2008
>
> Note: *RGE Monitor* is an economic analysis website (www.rgemonitor.com) founded by a group of economic and political experts.

Today, in the spring of 2009, after more than a year of cataclysmic economic occurrences, those who should know still don't have a clue as to what actually happened or why it occurred. In congressional hearings on October 23, 2008, Representative Henry Waxman asked Mr. Greenspan, "In other words, you found that your view of the world, your ideology was not right. It was not working." The maestro replied, "Precisely. That's precisely the reason I was shocked, because I had been going for forty years or more with very considerable evidence that it was working exceptionally well. . . . I still do not fully understand why it [the crisis] happened."[9]

Economist Jeff Madrick, a sharp critic of his mainstream colleagues, attended the December 2008 annual meeting of the American Economic Association in San Francisco and found that no one took any blame for failing to foresee what was happening. No one suggested that something must be wrong with a discipline that had no idea that a very severe recession, or a possible depression, was striking, fast and without mercy.[10] The irony is that some of the very same people whose heads were in the sand—except when they were up and about sniffing for easy money to be made—are now in charge of the government's unprecedented bailout. No wonder the people are up in arms.

So, then, we have an economy sailing along, poised, it seemed, for even better things to come, and all of a sudden the wheels fall off the bus. The economists and financiers can't tell us what happened or why it happened. Their training doesn't seem to have prepared them for this.[11] If ever there was a time when the emperor had no clothes, it is now. What are we to do in such circumstances? Was it all a big accident? Were evil men and women conspiring to ruin the economy, while they enriched themselves? Was it Bush's fault? Clinton's? Greenspan's? Here are some good starting suggestions for those of you who want to find out. Ignore what you see on television. Don't listen to or read the commentaries of mainstream economists. Hide your wallet when bankers or Wall Street bigwigs put forth their two cents. Assume that when government spokespersons are at the podium that they are either lying or ignorant of the truth. And most important, *Read on!*

2. What Makes Capitalism Tick?

Accumulate! Accumulate! That is Moses and the Prophets.
—KARL MARX, 1867

A working person toiling away on an automobile assembly line or in a restaurant kitchen must have found it difficult to understand how the bankers and brokers who have brought the economy to its knees made so much money simply by selling pieces of paper. If workers make cars, houses, or meals or teach children, and when farmers produce food, they are producing something that people need and can use. But those who sell complex financial instruments don't produce anything tangible at all. Something doesn't seem right about making money without producing a useful good or service. And indeed, no society can survive if the only economic activity—or even the dominant activity—is lending and borrowing money. The same can be said for buying already-made things at one price and selling them at a higher price. If the only economic activity is merchant trade, everyone will soon die because nothing is being produced. At its most fundamental level, an economy is a system of production of at least some useful outputs. When so much labor is devoted to the buying and selling of pieces of paper, with the sole aim of converting money into money, something profoundly irrational is taking place.

Every society must organize its land, raw materials, tools, and labor (together these are called the means of production) so that when combined, food, clothing, and shelter are brought into being. For most of our time on earth we organized our small societies collectively to produce things and shared what we made in a roughly equal way. We no longer do this, but we still produce, as we must. Our system of production is called *capitalism,* and inside it, a relatively small number of people, called capitalists, control the organization of the means of production—through their ownership of everything but the labor—with the aim of getting the output made in such a way that they make as much money as possible. The way it works is pretty simple.[12] The majority of people do not own enough land, materials, and the like to produce what they need for themselves. So they must sell the one thing they do have—their ability to work—to the owners of businesses. Once sold, our labor becomes the property of our employers. Since most of us have no alternative way to survive except to work for somebody, we enter into a profoundly unequal relationship with our employers, one that allows them to organize production to their advantage. They are able to compel us to work a number of hours and in such ways so as to yield them a surplus above their costs. This surplus output is theirs because they are the owners, and when they sell it, the money is their profit, to do with as they please. They claim that this is their just return for the use of their money and their management skills. But the real source of profits is our hard work.

To put matters bluntly, profits are the result of the exploitation of the workers. In other words, employers own the entire process and use this control to extract a surplus from the work of their employees. What is more, during the workday the employers own our ability to work, and they have the power and the legal right to continually change the way in which we labor and the tools and machines with which we work. They divide our labor into details that involve as little skill as possible to economize on skilled labor and utilize the enormous pool of persons capable of doing lower-paid unskilled work. They introduce machines to replace us and further dilute our skills. Both of these initiatives, by reducing the need for skill and by substituting machines for workers, help to create a *reserve army of labor,* a group of people in the precarious situation of going from being unemployed to employed and back again with relative ease. They can be called upon when needed during economic upswings and discarded during downturns. Their presence puts downward pressure on the wages of those already working. All of this makes the large number of people in the reserve pool of labor critical to the employer's ability to make money.

Once profits have been realized through the sale of the output, the owners have to decide what to do with the extra money after paying all costs. They could spend it recklessly on lavish consumption. They could give it to their workers or to charity. Some lavish consumption certainly occurs and so do gifts to charity—the latter helps to elevate the social status of the wealthy. But each business faces competitors, either currently in the market or threatening to enter it. Competition forces firms to deploy their profits judiciously, with an eye toward making their enterprises more efficient, expanding the market, and gaining a larger share of it. This need to grow, to expand the invested capital, is what is meant by the *accumulation of capital.* Making profits and accumulating ever greater amounts of personal wealth is the driving force of capitalism, and it accounts for capitalism's great dynamism, its technological aggressiveness, and its tendency to move beyond its starting point, both in terms of the product mix and geographical scope of a given company. Businesses may begin locally, producing a single good or service. Before long, however, successful firms produce many things and soon operate on a national and then an international scale. As a report for the Grocery Manufacturers Association in the United States clearly put it: "The case for global expansion is quite simple. As domestic markets are saturated, global expansion is one way to achieve sustainable, double-digit growth."

While making money through the accumulation of capital means the exploitation of workers, the degradation of their labor, and the creation of an enormous pool of surplus workers, at least it produces some necessary goods and services. But once capitalism gets rolling, it brings with it—and encourages—many new ways (and reinvigorates some old ways) of making money without bothering with production. Capitalist economies are money economies; they revolve around buying and selling. Once they begin to mature, the importance increases of all sorts of businesses that make money by purely financial transactions: banks, insurance companies, stock and bond brokerages, exchanges for buying and selling foreign currencies, and so forth. Alongside the *real* economy of production, a *financial* economy arises and begins to take on a life of its own, not always connected to the world of production. The independent development of the financial economy adds, as we shall see, new layers of irrationality to the system. What happens in finance can adversely affect the real economy, and crises in the latter can lead to changes in finance that reverberate back to the world of production with disastrous consequences.

We must make an important point here: *There is a close connection between politics and the drive to accumulate capital.* The owners of the largest businesses have come to exert great political influence. This is not surprising, given the importance of the production they control and the wealth this brings them. Politicians need large sums of money to run for and stay in office, and this alone makes them beholden to those who have it—the owners of large industrial corporations, banks, and other big firms. The owners use their influence with the government to keep workers in line (the British government once made joining a union a crime, and in the United States, the law, courts, and politicians have put many obstacles in the way of union organizing) and remove any barriers to accumulation, including, most critically, impediments put in place by weaker countries that limit foreign investment and resource removal.

The history of accumulation has been from its beginning about the penetration of Africa, Latin America, and Asia by the first capitalist nations: England, Holland, France, Belgium, Italy, Germany, and the United States. (Some countries, such as Spain, were important and brutal colonizers, but they were not capitalist until much later. Much of the wealth they stole from their colonies went to pay debts to England. Other nations, notably Japan, joined the imperialist club later.) The theft of peasant lands and mineral wealth, along with the slave trade and plantation agriculture, greatly stimulated the initial capital accumulation and made possible the full flowering of early capitalism. Today rich countries continue to dominate poor ones, though the ways in which they do so are more indirect than in the colonial era, relying on local political elites to see to it that wages are kept low and that favorable trade agreements are negotiated. Poor countries are politically independent but economically subservient to their rich counterparts. The relationship between Mexico and the United States is a case in point.

Anyone who doubts the close and corrupting connection between business interests and the political process should read Simon Johnson's "The Quiet Coup," in the May 2009 issue of *The Atlantic Monthly*. Johnson, a professor at MIT and former chief economist at the International Monetary Fund, has described the depth of the corruption inherent in the cozy connection between the fabulously wealthy and the government, and the consequences for the economy and society:

> The great wealth that the financial sector created and concentrated gave bankers enormous political weight—a weight not seen in the U.S. since the era of J. P. Morgan (the man). In that period, the banking panic of 1907 could be stopped only by coordination among private-sector bankers: no government entity was able to offer an effective response. But that first age of banking oligarchs came to an end with the passage of significant banking regulation in response to the Great Depression; the reemergence of an American financial oligarchy is quite recent.

3. Capitalist Economies Are Prone to Crises

Capitalism's instability is systemic.

—RICHARD WOLFF, 2008

As we noted in the last chapter, capitalist economies are defined by the following characteristics:

- Most of society's productive resources—land, raw materials, machinery, factory buildings—are owned by a small percentage of the population.
- Most people have no way to live but to sell their capacity to work—their labor power—to the highest bidder.
- Relentless profit seeking by business owners.
- Reliance by most people on wage work in order to live.

Although there is much planning within individual capitalist corporations, capitalist economies as a whole are unplanned. What happens with respect to the mix of products produced and the amount of unutilized labor, for example, is the result of decisions made by millions of sellers and buyers. Mainstream economists say that even though production is unplanned, people's needs are still satisfied in capitalism, and, ironically, this happens because the buyers and sellers seek only their own interests. They supposedly meet in the marketplace, and competition among them ensures that things will proceed smoothly. All the goods and services needed by people will be automatically provided. As Adam Smith put it: "It is not from the benevolence of the butcher, the brewer, or the baker that we expect our dinner, but from their regard to their own interest." If there is a lack of some product, the price will go up as people compete to purchase it, encouraging businesses to produce more. If consumers want less of something, they don't buy as much, and prices decrease. Some businesses will fail, reducing supply, which is what consumers wanted. Thus the needs and wants of all people can be satisfied by the workings of the market, by consumers and the owners of businesses responding to the "signals" or "cues" that the market sends.

There are many reasons to believe that the mainstream understanding of capitalism is a myth. If it were true that a capitalist economy more or less automatically guarantees maximum public welfare, how can this be squared with what history clearly teaches us, for example, that the system is unable to provide jobs for all those who must work to earn money to purchase the necessities of life. Even in the best of times, millions are unemployed. What is more, having a job really isn't enough, because many low-wage workers don't earn enough to allow them to meet their families' basic needs for shelter, clothing, food, medical care, and so on. Increases in the federal minimum wage have rarely kept up with inflation; the purchasing power of the minimum wage is significantly less now than it was in the 1960s and 1970s, and is less than the official—and meager—poverty level of income for a family of three. More than a quarter of all jobs pay a wage that would not support a family of four at this level.[13]

We could go on about the shortcomings of mainstream economics. Suffice it to say that most economists did not think that a crisis such as the current one could happen at all. And if by some remarkable and unpredictable chain of events one did occur, the "magic of the marketplace" would soon correct things and restore order. Such nonsense suggests that it is time to abandon the "common wisdom" and look elsewhere to unlock how capitalism actually works in the real world.

Economic data indicate that, sooner or later, capital accumulation comes up against obstacles that slows it down or stops it altogether. These disruptions of the accumulation process are called *crises.* A short period of such disruption is called a *recession*, while a longer, deeper downturn is called a *depression*. Recessions occur with some regularity, while depressions are much rarer. Right now we are in a deep recession, which might become a depression. Japan experienced a severe recession, probably better characterized as a long stagnation (very slow growth) for the entire decade of the 1990s. Since the Second World War, there have been many recessions: in the late 1940s, late 1950s, mid-1970s, a severe one in the early 1980s, early 1990s, early 2000s, and now the present one, which started toward the end of 2007. The worst depression was the Great Depression, which lasted for more than ten years and ended only with the massive government spending of the Second World War. All told, since the mid-1850s there have been thirty-two recessions or depressions in the United States—with the average contraction lasting around a year and a half and the average expansion between contractions lasting about nine years. Both recessions and depressions are often associated with financial panics and breakdowns; sometimes these are causal factors, sometimes consequences, sometimes both cause and effect.

In the often-quoted beginning of *Anna Karenina*, Tolstoy writes, "Happy families are all alike; every unhappy family is unhappy in its own way." Downturns in the economy (and the financial crises that sometimes accompany them) have some common traits, but they also have their own unique histories and characteristics. We have already commented on the differences between the present recession and that of 1982. We have also noted the likelihood that during periods of expansion a capitalist economy without any planning mechanism will develop excess production capacity and produce too much, forcing a cutback in production and employment. (This is happening to the automobile industry, which developed huge excess capacity—amounting to about 50 percent—both in the United States and globally.)

It should come as no surprise that recessions, depressions, and crises occur in an economic system in which businesses follow their own financial interests without coordination or planning for society's needs. What we might call ordinary business cycles occur when, during boom years, companies expand employment and production to keep up with increasing demand, but, not anticipating any slowdown, end up with an overabundance of stuff to sell. They then decrease production and lay off workers, setting off a recession. When production and demand come back in balance, the process repeats itself.

There are also other ways in which accumulation can be interrupted. Mainstream economists believe that deep recessions and even depressions are always caused by some traumatic event or set of events that strike the economy from the "outside." Although we believe the opposite, that capitalist economies are by their nature prone to crises, outside forces can certainly generate economic difficulties. If a large bank suddenly and unexpectedly fails, its relationships with borrowers could cause problems significant enough to negatively affect the entire economy. No doubt the swift 2008 invasion of the Republic of Georgia by Russia slowed down accumulation in Georgia. The devastating earthquakes and tsunami that struck Indonesia in 2004 retarded that nation's economic growth. If speculators attack a country's currency so that its value falls in relation to other currencies, the rise in the price of imports that this brings about (if, for example, it takes more dollars to buy yen, then Japanese goods will be more expensive in the United States) could lower the rate of capital accumulation. That is, the growth of the economy will slow down.

However, we do not think that unexpected events originating externally are the main danger as far as capital accumulation is concerned. We contend that the very process of capital accumulation itself, naturally and without fail, brings along with it long-term and intractable barriers to the generation of profits and capital growth. There are several possibilities here. As businesses replace workers with machines, production becomes ever more "capital intensive."

The purpose of automation is to make it possible to produce more with less labor. After one company makes a breakthrough in substituting machines for labor, lowering the cost to produce something, other companies making the same commodity must do the same if they are to remain in business. In an economy characterized by free competition as in the nineteenth century, companies making similar goods or providing the same services are in a competition for people to buy what they sell. Competition to sell a greater supply pushes prices down. This means that, over time, there is less labor per unit of machinery to exploit, and at the same time prices are falling. It follows that the rate of profit on the invested capital falls as well. Declining profits decrease capital accumulation, because employers will be less likely to invest in making more of the same product when profits are lower. During a recession, when it becomes harder to sell products, some firms will go under, in effect destroying capital and restoring higher profitability for the remaining businesses when the economy rebounds.

A second possibility, and the one we want to emphasize, is the result of the interaction between two tendencies of mature capitalist economies: the tendency for production to be dominated by relatively few companies and the tendency for insufficient investment opportunities in production of goods or services. We think that this barrier to accumulation is significant enough to warrant a separate chapter.

4. Mature Capitalism's Concentration of Production and Slow Growth

The normal tendency of capitalism in its monopoly stage [is] one of economic stagnation due to the inability to absorb the enormous actual and potential surplus at its disposal. Given a tendency to stagnation in monopoly capitalism, what need[s] to be explained [is] not stagnation as much as prosperity.

—JOHN BELLAMY FOSTER, 2005

In mature capitalist economies, such as those of the United States, Japan, and Germany, capital accumulation involves a rising *concentration of production*, that is, a tendency for production and markets to be dominated by a relatively small number of very large firms. Business owners are always trying to eliminate rivals, both to increase their share of the market and to increase their power to raise prices without the fear that consumers will go elsewhere. "Only the strong survive," as the saying goes. How many automobile companies are there worldwide? Steel corporations? Pharmaceutical businesses? When a large number of small firms has been winnowed down to a much smaller number of giant corporations, we say that markets can be described by the word *oligopoly* (the prefix *oli* means "a few"). Such firms are said to have considerable "monopoly power" so it is also possible to call them quasi-monopolies or even monopoly capital. Steep recessions and depressions are especially good times for strong companies to gain market share from weaker ones and eventually force them out of business.

The second tendency, ***a shortage of investment outlets in the productive economy,*** can be illustrated by a capsule history of advanced capitalist production. Capitalism went through various stages as it grew and developed. During the initial period of industrial capitalism in the early to mid-1800s, there was a great amount of investment demand (or stimulus, to use a contemporary word). Capitalism was in its buildup phase—factories of many kinds were built; equipment to supply the factories and trading ships were manufactured; canals were dug for easier transport within countries; and trade abroad brought growth. Imperialism in its colonial phase helped to provide a steady source of raw materials, and markets to sell some of the new industrial products. The building of the railroad systems provided an economic lift during construction, and more so afterward because of the much cheaper overland shipment of goods railroads made possible. Railroads also encouraged the settling of the interior of the United States in the late 1800s and early 1900s. This spurred agricultural and industrial development in the heartland. During this period, there were "normal" business cycle recessions, as well as depressions—occurring mainly as a result of the growth of production getting ahead of what could actually be sold. But at the same time, there were many stimulants to the economy.

In mature capitalist economies, however, there is typically a problem of slow growth, or stagnation. The normal condition for much of the last half-century has been one of much slower growth than the system is capable of delivering. Factories have already been built, as has much of the infrastructure—from roads to water systems to electric power lines, and so on. (Although it is true that much of this infrastructure in the United States is in a sorry state of disrepair and needs rebuilding.) Growth is occurring, but at relatively low levels.

In other words, in countries like the United States, there are more than enough buildings, tools, machines, roads, bridges, and ports to help produce a very large output. So, there are fewer new investment opportunities than during earlier periods of capitalist production.

The first feature of capitalist maturity—the concentration of production—raises profits and at the same time reinforces the second feature—the lack of investment opportunities. Then the interaction of these two conditions creates the conditions that lead to stagnation. A large corporation in an oligopolistic market, such as Toyota, has already made enormous investments. It has a sophisticated managerial structure and research capacity, geared to constantly reduce costs. In modern auto plants, work has been structured in such a way that workers can be compelled to labor fifty-seven out of every sixty seconds. Wal-Mart is so large and powerful that it can do the same thing and can also demand low prices from its suppliers. Wal-Mart has built huge growth on low prices—but can profit at those low prices because it has the power to squeeze suppliers and, in a relatively weak economy, pay low wages. Large oligopolistic companies have learned to keep their inventories at an absolute minimum, lowering costs even more. Such gargantuan companies are protected by their market power from having to endure cutthroat price competition from rivals, each of which may fear a price war that will ruin all of them. Each has too much capital invested to risk this. Their large size makes it difficult for new firms to enter the market to compete.

One more thing of importance here is that large corporations will not very likely be willing to scrap their considerable physical capital to build more efficient plants until the old buildings and machinery wear out. Such a move would be too costly from their point of view. Thus in oligopolistic industries, there will be plenty of old plants existing side by side with newer plants and equipment. The profit margins are so high in these industries in good times that it is possible to operate profitably even with old technology. But from the perspective of the national economy, the slowness with which new capital comes on line means that investment outlets are all the more constrained. By contrast, in the more competitive era before the rise of oligopolies, machines and equipment were often scrapped as soon as a new technique of production became known. This meant that large amounts of investment—purchases of newly produced capital goods—went hand in hand with technological innovation, keeping capital accumulation robust. With oligopolies this no longer happens.

To summarize: In mature capitalist economies, investment outlets diminish as capital saturation of the major industries sets in. Oligopolies further reduce investment by refusing to scrap older, less efficient facilities. At the same time, growing concentration of production, what is called *monopoly capitalism*, generates a rising surplus of profits in the hands of giant corporations. This surplus capital needs to be reinvested if accumulation is to continue at a rapid pace. But if the standard investment outlets are not growing as swiftly as the rising surplus, then accumulation will slow down and the growth of the society's output will decrease (and, as we will see, the wealthy begin a search for other ways to make money). This will continue until and unless there are new and growing outlets for the surplus in the productive economy. Meanwhile, the economy cannot achieve its potential growth rate. A long period of stagnation means that the gap between what could be produced and what is produced grows larger.[14]

5. Can the Tendency to Slow Growth Be Overcome?

Epoch-making inventions shake up the entire pattern of the economy and hence create investment outlets in addition to the capital which they directly absorb.

—PAUL BARAN and PAUL SWEEZY, 1966

To say that there is a tendency to something implies that it can be overcome if certain things happen. If a person has a tendency toward obesity, that person can counter this tendency by maintaining a strict lower daily caloric intake and exercise more. But if the countermeasure stops, the tendency will reassert itself. Can the tendency of mature capitalist economies to grow slowly (stagnate) be countered? Let's look at some possibilities.

In their book *Monopoly Capital* radical economists Paul Baran and Paul Sweezy provide one of the most sophisticated elaborations of the stagnation tendency of economies like that of the United States. In describing the most powerful counter-effect to this tendency, the *epoch-making innovation,* they identify three historical instances of it: the steam engine, the railroad, and the automobile. During the twentieth century, the most important investment-generating innovation was the automobile. The mass production and sale of automobiles and trucks brought with it extraordinarily large amounts of investment. Consider the Lordstown, Ohio, plant of General Motors. The plant itself is a vast agglomeration of capital—buildings, tools, machinery, and the like. The plant has extensive and complex arrangements with many firms that supply parts or completely assembled components, such as front seats. There is a vast network of GM dealers that sell and service the cars. If we consider the industry in general, automobiles have been investment-generating dynamos. Millions of miles of highways and paved streets, hundreds of thousands of bridges, oil and gasoline, glass, steel, suburban development made possible by cars, motels, hotels, restaurants, and scores of other businesses were made profitable by the automobile. First in the 1920s and later after the Second World War, brisk demand for cars and trucks propelled the economy forward. It is interesting to note that today the nation is saturated with automobiles and the industry is no longer the engine of growth it once was. Even Toyota, the titan of the global car industry, is in trouble. What will take the place of the automobile in the early twenty-first century as an engine of prolonged economic growth?

When domestic outlets for surplus funds are limited, will foreign investment do the trick? When U.S. companies build plants in China, they may spend some of their profits (though the Chinese government may actually do the building, or the U.S. entity may raise funds in China and spend nothing). However, if demand for the products made in China is robust, low Chinese wages and taxes will make profits still greater, again re-creating the same problem of how to profitably utilize the surplus.

A major conflict, such as the Second World War, can absorb monumental amounts of surplus, as can military spending in general. However, unless the government itself produces war materials on a nonprofit basis, such public outlays invariably enrich private companies, creating more surplus that will need to be absorbed (find investment outlets) in the future. Consider the tens of billions of dollars of profits that filled the coffers of Haliburton and other favored contractors during the wars initiated by the United States following the events of September 11, 2001. In addition, modern wars, such as that in Iraq, are not on a scale large enough to be the equivalent of the automobile and railroad. What is more, a nation at war risks devastating destruction of its capital and death to its people, as well as people in other countries.

What about civilian government spending? Could the government levy taxes on some of the surplus (or borrow it by issuing and selling government bonds) and then invest the money itself, but in public capital projects? This is what the great liberal economist John Maynard Keynes said could end the Great Depression. There are possibilities here but problems as well. The government spending best suited to deal with a rising surplus and a lack of private investment outlets would be on projects that do not themselves raise the surplus. For example, there is a huge amount of substandard housing in the United States and a need for good cheap new housing. Imagine that the government stood ready to spend five hundred billion dollars to attack the housing problem. Let's say a public corporation is established to plan and build housing complexes, rehab old housing, and train workers to perform the labor. Assume that housing units can be built for $50,000 apiece and that 80 percent of the money is used to create new housing. Four hundred billion dollars would build eight million housing units—at three persons per unit these could house twenty-four million people. The rest of the money would be for planning, training workers, and rehabbing already existing units. A public mortgage bank could be established to make low-interest loans to home buyers. A wonderful idea, isn't it? Yes, it is, but it misses entirely the political reality of capitalism. Capitalists would raise a storm of protest against this public encroachment on the private sector, which, if successful, would greatly reduce their ability to make money in the housing market. Their many flunkies in Congress and the media would rail against this "socialist" nonsense. Of course, if there was a massive, strong, and militant labor movement willing to take to the streets to support and defend such a program, it might have a chance. This is something to remember as we develop our arguments further in the next chapter. If there is no movement to force the government to absorb the surplus and make socially useful public expenditures, then the government will only do things that maintain the current system and its relationships, and in the end this will tend to keep surplus (profits) high relative to investment outlets, perpetuating the stagnation problem.

When investments in the real economy are not profitable enough to justify themselves, capitalists have tried to deal with the predicament of stagnation by developing new ways to utilize the surplus and make money, especially doing so without making any product or providing any service. But, as we will see, this quest has led to one calamity after another: stock market crashes, bursting bubbles, recessions, and depressions. The current crisis that started in 2007 was set off by the fall of housing prices after the growth of a huge real estate bubble.

6. Economic Stagnation Sets in Following the Second World War

Let me . . . point out that the fact that the overall performance of the economy in recent years has not been much worse than it actually has been, or as bad as it was in the 1930s, is largely owing to three causes: (1) the much greater role of government spending and government deficits; (2) the enormous growth of consumer debt, including residential mortgage debt, especially during the 1970s; and (3) the ballooning of the financial sector of the economy, which, apart from the growth of debt as such, includes an explosion of all kinds of speculation, old and new, which in turn generates more than a mere trickle-down of purchasing power into the "real" economy, mostly in the form of increased demand for luxury goods. These are important forces counteracting stagnation as long as they last, but there is always the danger that if carried too far they will erupt in an old-fashioned panic of a kind we haven't seen since the 1929–33 period.

—PAUL SWEEZY, 1982

We can illustrate our arguments concretely by looking at some modern U.S. economic history. Our analysis tells us that a period of very high growth must be due to some extraordinary source of investment demand, one that fully counteracts the tendency toward stagnation. One such period was the Second World War. During the war there were three years (1941, 1942, and 1943) when the annual real growth of the economy exceeded 16 percent, and growth exceeded 8 percent in three other years (1939, 1940, and 1944). The enormous government spending for the war effort ignited and maintained this rapid growth, for the military needed everything—from clothes to food to guns and ammunition to jeeps and trucks and tanks, to temporary housing, airplanes, ships, and so on. The long depression of the 1930s melted away in the face of such tremendous investment. But it took extraordinary circumstances, a massive war effort, with unprecedented government spending financed by borrowing, for this to happen. Without these, the economy would have continued to stagnate, with very high unemployment and low growth.

The U.S. economy grew less rapidly after the war but still at a fairly high clip. GDP growth slowed to around 4 percent in the 1950s and 1960s, low by 1940s standards but still respectably high. (See Table 1 for decade-by-decade growth rates.) These relatively high growth rates occurred for a number of reasons. There was considerable pent-up demand because during the war many consumer goods, including automobiles, were not available or were sharply rationed. This meant that households were forced to save money, and this created pent-up demand that could only be realized after the war. The United States was the only major participant in the war whose physical capital was not destroyed or damaged. As countries rebuilt their economies, they were forced to buy every conceivable good and resource from the United States, leading to an export boom. In addition, the automobile had its greatest effect on the economy during this period, as suburbs were built, the extensive interstate highway system constructed, and hotels, restaurants, gas stations, auto repair shops, and the like were built to meet the needs and desires of a more mobile population. Government spending was not cut back to prewar levels, and in fact, led by rising defense spending, grew steadily, adding to total demand. It also funded programs that subsidized home ownership and college education, leading to investments in these important sectors. There were also innovations in consumer credit, and household debt helped to prop up demand. So, unique forces were at work after the war, as there were during it, to help maintain high demand and growth rates. This provided capitalists out-

TABLE 1: *Growth in real GDP 1930–2008 (corrected for inflation)*[15]

	Average annual percent growth in real GDP
1930s	1.3
1940s	5.9
1950s	4.1
1960s	4.4
1970s	3.3
1980s	3.1
1990s	3.1
2000–2008	2.2

lets for their investments in the economy of real goods and services. The problem was that these forces could not be sustained indefinitely.

The rapid capital accumulation of the war and the first two postwar decades began to run into obstacles, as all such accumulation must, in the 1970s. The world was now flush with factories, tools, and machinery, all the end products of the investments made during the boom. Thus profitable investment opportunities became harder to find. At the same time, U.S. corporations were beginning to face serious competition from Japan and Germany, both of which had rebuilt and enlarged their productive capacity with the most technologically efficient capital. These countries also spent very little on defense, while the United States was waging a cold war against the Soviet Union and a hot one in Vietnam. Organized labor had grown, with some power both in manufacturing workplaces and in the political sphere. The United States did not have a European-style welfare state, but it had increased social welfare spending enough to make workers more secure than they had ever been. There was now unemployment compensation, Social Security, Medicare and Medicaid, food stamps, low-cost and free lunches for children at school, more public housing, and other forms of direct public assistance.

Slower growth has been the rule ever since, as Table 1 clearly shows. GDP increased by 3.3 percent per year in the 1970s, 3.1 percent in the 1980s and 1990s, and 2.2 percent from 2000 to 2008. Another sign of protracted slow growth has been the decline in capacity utilization in manufacturing. During the early 1970s, the percent of industrial capacity actually used for production was around 85 percent. By 1984, this was down to about 78 percent, and despite an increase starting in the mid-1990s, decreased consistently in the late 1990s and in the 2000s, and returned to about 78 percent in 2007. The rate of manufacturing capacity utilization as this is being written is 66 percent, the lowest since records started being kept in 1948.[16]

A serious problem was that the power of the automobile industry to drive the accumulation process began to wane, as the advanced capitalist countries started to become saturated with cars and trucks and the world's poor nations did not have a mass market large enough to take up the slack. Huge excess capacity in the industry in the United States, fueled in part by intense competition from Japanese producers who began to locate plants here, forced the closing of plants. The car companies have for years had the capacity to turn out close to 50 percent more cars than they did have. And today, of course, the U.S. auto companies are on government-sponsored life support as are most of those in Europe and Japan.

Another indication of the slowing of the economy is that following each post–Second World War recession there has been a definite trend of increasing time to recoup the jobs lost during the recession (see Table 2). Even when a huge percentage of jobs are not lost, as in the 2001 recession, it is taking the economy increasingly longer to produce enough jobs to make up for those lost in the downturn—four years for that one. Some states, such as Massachusetts, never did recover the jobs lost.

The trouble was that no other "epoch-making" innovation—great enough to propel the economy to prolonged high rates of growth—arose to replace the automobile. From the time in which the economy began to slow down in the mid-1970s, no technology or other force has come along with the transformative effect of stimulating growth like the railroads in the nineteenth century, the Second World War in the 1940s, or the automobile in the immediate postwar era. Even the widespread use of computers has not stimulated the economy to the

TABLE 2: *Jobs lost during post–Second World War recessions and time to regain lost jobs following end of downturn.*[17]

Date recession ended	Jobs lost as percentage of number employed at start of recession	Months needed to regain lost jobs
Oct. 1945	7.9	18
Oct. 1949	5.0	21
Apr. 1958	4.0	21
Mar. 1975	1.6	26
Apr. 1982	3.1	29
Mar. 1991	1.1	32
Nov. 2001	1.7	48
20—?	4.8 (through June 2009)	?

extent that the automobile once did. Although the manufacture of chips and computers uses factories and labor, there have been no noticeable spin-offs that increased the growth of the rest of the economy. In many cases, such as the use of computers and robots in factory production, the electronic revolution simply enhanced the efficiency of the system and decreased labor needs.

Nor did the U.S. wars against Afghanistan and Iraq take up the slack, although the massive resources, including the workers employed in war production and in carrying out the wars, have certainly helped keep the economy going. However, these have not stimulated economic growth anywhere close to what occurred in the Second World War, during which the mobilization of people and production was many times more massive.

As we argued above, slow growth reduces profits and this is what happened in the 1970s. Profits, as a percentage of the economy, began to decline. In the 1950s and 1960s, profits were in the range of 8 to over 10 percent of the Gross Domestic Product.[18] But the trend after this was downward, averaging a little over 5 percent for the first years of the 1980s.

7. Neoliberalism

There is no alternative.

—MARGARET THATCHER, early 1980s

Capitalists (here we are speaking of large stockholders and the officers of our largest corporations, those that wield the most economic and political power) are intolerant of any slowdown in growth that cuts into their profits, and as soon as these were noted in the 1970s and 1980s, capitalists began an aggressive campaign to maintain and even expand their profit margins—even if the economy as a whole was doing worse, and even if this would compound the economic problems. The state also got into the act on the behalf of capital and the rich, redistributing income and wealth from the poor to the rich, what Jesse Jackson was to call "Robin Hood in Reverse." All of this was justified as the way to get the economy going again. The immediate goal of course was to cut labor costs, but the long-term plan was to undo the New Deal programs and restore to the owners of capital greater control of the economy and enhance their ability to gain as much profit as possible. A primary weapon was ideological. Businesses and wealthy individual capitalists funded "think tanks" such as the Heritage Foundation and the American Enterprise Institute to wage a war of ideas against the welfare state, labor unions, big government, and any and all public regulation of businesses. According to the employers, these were the causes of the profit decline. Corporate America also consolidated and expanded its political operations, hiring lobbyists by the busload and filling the campaign coffers of politicians of both parties to push the new agenda in Congress, eventually accepted by liberals as well as conservatives. These efforts coalesced into what is known as *neoliberalism*, the politics of "free market" economics, which is a program that consists of these elements:[19]

- Eliminating all barriers to the movement of both physical and money capital, within a country and among all countries.

- Privatizing as much public enterprise as possible. The government is asserted to be inherently inefficient. Public employees are considered parasitic, earning high wages while doing little work.

- Tightening requirements for receiving any kind of assistance for the poor from the government, or ending welfare programs altogether, and at the same time making it easier for businesses to get money from governments.

- Cutting taxes on businesses, capital gains, and the incomes of the rich. This must be done because businesses and wealthy individuals are the sources of investment, economic growth, and jobs. Only if they prosper will the rest of us do okay.

- Making it more difficult for workers to form unions and bargain with employers. Unions are said to make markets less competitive and to encourage less work effort.

- Seeing inflation as a public scourge and making sure through the monetary policies of the central bank (the Federal Reserve in the United States) that inflation is kept at bay.

Neoliberalism hit full stride with the election of Ronald Reagan. He fired striking air traffic controllers, signaling to employers that the government would not stand in their way as they waged war on unions and workers. He filled worker-protection and civil rights agencies with reactionaries who made rulings contradicting the very purposes of the laws and regulations they were supposed to enforce. Over the twenty-eight-year period from 1980 to 2008, we have seen a relentless procession of anti-labor trade agreements, deregulation of one industry after another, privatizations, refusals to regulate new entities like hedge funds and complex financial instruments, and the shredding of the social safety net.

Three consequences of neoliberalism deserve mention at this point in our argument. First, as neoliberalism took hold, workers were squeezed, and squeezed hard. For already existing businesses, slashing costs became a primary way to enhance profits. Although businesses have always been forced to reduce costs as competitors used cost-saving procedures such as new and more efficient machines, there was an added need to do so after the mid-1970s because of slow economic growth. And one of the ways to become more "efficient" was to force workers to work harder for less. Reagan's anti-labor message told businesses that it was now politically acceptable to use hardball tactics to break unions and bust their strikes. So successful were employers (and so inept were the unions) that union membership declined from 23.5 percent in 1970 to 15.5 percent in 1990 and 12.4 percent in 2008—with much of the remaining union strength among government employees. Wal-Mart, the largest employer in the country, with 1.2 million workers, has made a special effort to stay union-free. Since union workers earn more money and have more and better benefits than do non-union employees, the successful corporate campaign against unions lowered business costs and increased profits.[20]

With the power of workers in decline, employers were able to attack key benefit costs, such as pensions and health care. They began to rid themselves of expensive defined pension plans (with specific amounts promised to retirees) and to replace them with defined contribution plans, which do not guarantee a specific pension payout and to which workers had to contribute some of their wages. Workers were also forced to pay for more of the costs of their health insurance. New employees often found themselves with neither a pension nor a health care plan.

As the power of capitalists grew at the expense of labor, the average wage stopped rising. When corrected for inflation, the average wage in 2006 was about 8 percent less than the peak reached in 1972 and about the same as it was in the late 1960s. Greater amounts of company income were directed toward profits (or astronomically large salaries for top management) instead of wages, resulting in wages and salaries becoming smaller relative to the economy (GDP). This led to a much greater inequality of income—by 2006 the top 1 percent of households received close to a quarter of all income and the top 10 percent got 50 percent of the income pie. In 2006, the 400 richest Americans had a collective net worth of $1.6 trillion, more than the combined wealth of the bottom 150 million people. This degree of income and wealth inequality was last seen just before the beginning of the Great Depression.[21]

Another way that business owners sought to divert more income into profits was to make do with fewer workers. The new management mantra became "do more with less," or what worker advocates called "management by stress." The success of this strategy was part of the reason for the weak job growth during the recovery from the 2001 recession. But doing more with fewer workers just means that the remaining workers must work harder. During this period, from 2000 through 2007, as the volume of manufacturing products increased, the number of manufacturing workers declined by some three million.[22] This indicates greatly increased labor productivity. But the benefits of this rising productivity went mainly to management and business owners and not to workers. It was also during this period that many jobs were transferred to other countries—mainly in Asia—as outsourcing of manufacturing and services accelerated. As public affairs journalist Bill Moyers wrote about the worsening conditions of labor in the early 2000s: "Our business and political class owes us better than this. After all, it was they who declared class war twenty years ago, and it was they who won. They're on top."[23]

As workers found themselves less secure, with stagnant wages and great financial burdens, two things happened. They became more susceptible to the notion that each person is responsible for his or her own financial security. This seemed reasonable to many people when there was prosperity. In the late 1990s, when the stock market was on a rampage, workers followed the market and counted their newfound wealth in rapidly appreciating 401(k)s. A decade later, they did the same thing with their houses. However, money insecurity also led to rapid increases in household debt, as workers used credit cards to maintain their standards of living, including their health. They also borrowed against their homes. Financial institutions made mountains of cash loaning money to working men and women. In effect, those at the top extracted income from those below and then loaned some of this money back to those with lower incomes. On the one hand, debt allowed consumption to remain high and this added to the growth of the GDP. On the other hand, rising debt could not be sustained forever when the income that allowed the debt to be serviced (paying interest and principal) was not also rising.

A second effect of neoliberalism—spread through much of the world—was a rapid expansion in international trade and capital flows. Trade agreements (such as the North American Free Trade Agreement) and deregulation of global markets led to an increase in international financial transactions. Foreign currencies have to be bought and sold during trade transactions and investment. If a corporation in the United States wants to operate in Europe, it will need euros. This, in turn, will make U.S. businesses think about changes in the dollar-euro exchange rate; if the euros they now hold diminish in value compared to the dollar, they will get fewer dollars when they seek to convert foreign earnings back into dollars—that is, exchange foreign money for dollars that can be brought back and spent in the United States. This kind of thinking led to the creation of markets for financial instruments that allow the holder to hedge against harmful exchange-rate movements. Similar instruments were created to protect the holders against adverse changes in interest rates in different countries. As neoliberalism was embraced by governments around the world, capitalists saw profit opportunities in the so-called emerging markets, such as Brazil, Thailand, and Indonesia. Investments in these countries required special attention to risk, both political (sudden changes in governments) and economic (speculators rapidly selling off a currency in anticipation of political turmoil, for example). So, as global trade and business operations grew, financial transactions began to grow rapidly. The banks and other financial organizations that oversaw such transactions profited from these and began to see the possibility of making a lot more money.

A third result of neoliberalism derived from its attention to inflation, which included the suppression of wages and benefits. This created the kind of market stability in the United States conducive to the purchase of securities (stocks and bonds). The longest bull market in U.S. history took off in the middle of the 1980s, lasting until the technology stock bubble burst in 2000. Stocks provided a repository for the growing surplus taken from workers by capitalists as pension and worker 401(k) plans invested heavily. There were breaks in the upward movement of stock prices, some serious, especially the record fall in the Dow Jones index on October 19, 1987, but overall the trend was up, up, and up. Such a long bull market inevitably gives rise to notions that stock prices cannot fall, or if they do suffer a downward "correction," they will rise again soon. This in turn encourages nascent entrepreneurs, with the help of investment banks, to issue stocks for new enterprises. People, including leading economists, believed that a new economy had arisen—immune to major setbacks. In a period of stock market euphoria, various kinds of swindles also crop up. A "get rich quick" mentality seeps into the people's consciousness, and we will believe almost anything. A cottage industry of books, websites, advisors, and the like develops. When the computer technology revolution hit full stride in the 1990s, with real impact on the way in which business is conducted, the stock markets were ready for an accelerated bull market. The stock prices of many tech companies skyrocketed, even when the corporations had not yet made a profit. It was said that the prices reflected future profits, but since these are unknowable, what was really happening was mass delusion. A popular book of the time was titled *Dow 36,000*: the authors predicted a steady rise in the Dow to an astronomically high 36,000. This seems ludicrous today when the Dow has been well below 10,000 for many months.

The explosion of financial markets, to which we now turn, has a dual character. On the one hand, the growing prominence of such markets is due to the reassertion of slow growth or stagnation tendencies in the 1970s. While growing trade, foreign investment, and purchases of foreign stocks and bonds required an expansion of finance, financial markets also provided a convenient and profitable repository for the growing hoards of money that could not find profitable outlets in the real economy, that is, in investment in productive capacity and services.

On the other hand, the financial explosion helped to prop up demand and employment in the real economy. The inflation in stock prices gave rise to a *wealth effect*. As household wealth rose (as a result of higher stock prices), consumers were richer, at least on paper, than they had been and therefore felt they could save less and spend more. What is more, stocks can be borrowed against. And the perception of greater wealth can make households more willing to take on debt. During the housing bubble, the same things happened. So, consumption spurs the production of output, whether of luxury automobiles and yachts or housing construction materials. The trouble is that this process will go into reverse when asset prices stop rising.

One final point: financial institutions, whether they be ordinary commercial banks, investment banks, brokerages, hedge funds, equity capital funds, or the financing arms of automobile companies, all sell products—mortgages, stocks, bonds, auto loans, and so forth. To make more money and to compete effectively, financial firms must constantly market their products and invent new ones. Much of the work in finance is selling, and the salesperson here is just as conniving as the guy who tries to sell you a car or the broker who wants you to buy that house. The point of new financial instruments is invariably to get people to take on more risk by buying speculative products that promise high yields while at the same time suggesting that these are relatively risk-free. Deception is as common at a big brokerage as it is at your local auto dealer or real estate agency. History tells us, however, that the hard sell works, especially when markets are robust.

8. The Financial Explosion: Introduction

> *In every stockjobbing swindle everyone knows that some time or other the crash must come, but everyone hopes that it may fall on the head of his neighbor, after he himself has caught the shower of gold and placed it in safety.* Après moi le déluge! *is the watchword of every capitalist and of every capitalist nation. Hence Capital is reckless of the health or length of life of the laborer, unless under compulsion from society.*
>
> —KARL MARX, 1867

Even before capitalism existed, there were people who made money without making a product.[24] More than two thousand years ago, Aristotle referred to the making of money with money (buying a product and selling it for a higher price or loaning money in return for payment of interest as well as the original amount of principal) as "unnatural." This is now, of course, considered to be very "natural," and retail merchants, banks, and other financial businesses are all respected and important parts of capitalist economies.

The financial system used to be a relatively small, though important, sector of the capitalist economy. It helped economic growth by loaning money to businesses for expansion, new operations, and for operating capital. The creation of stock certificates helped businesses to raise money by allowing the ownership of companies to be divided up and sold. Insurance was sold to protect businesses and individuals from catastrophic losses. But what occurred in the last few decades, as capitalists were trying to find new ways to make profits, was the extraordinary expansion of the financial system, which absorbed a huge amount of capital (cash) that could have been spent on new businesses that produced goods or services but was not because of low profit expectations. Making money without actually making something turned out to be the largest growth sector of the U.S. economy from the early 1980s to the present crisis.

The explosive growth of finance did lead to increased employment. But employment in finance did not grow nearly as fast as its effect on the economy. In 2006, the financial sector employed about 6 percent of workers but "produced" 40 percent of all the profits of domestic industries. In 1960, by contrast, the FIRE sector of the economy (which includes strictly financial firms, insurance companies, and real estate) accounted for about 15 percent of the profits of all domestic firms. (In New York City between 2003 and 2007 the securities industry accounted for 59 percent of the growth in wages and salaries though composed of just 6 percent of private sector employment.)[25]

The growth of finance was greatly aided by the deregulation of global markets, referred to above. Through political negotiations that occurred in the late 1980s, the world's richest nations developed a framework for opening up the world to the financial companies of the leading capitalist countries, something not inevitably decreed by the marketplace but done so the wealthy could make still more money. The World Trade Organization's "Understanding on Commitments in Financial Services" made it much easier to make money with money abroad and to bring profits back to the home country as desired. The WTO did this primarily by prohibiting member nations from regulating financial transactions. All of the complex and ultimately lethal financial instruments discussed below could be sold anywhere, immune from government regulation. Companies like Citibank—which exemplified this global expansion, with 1,400 branch offices in forty-seven countries, including ten in Latin America, twenty-two in

Pacific Asia, and one in Africa (Egypt)—took advantage of the new trade agreements by selling toxic assets wherever it could, making as much money as it could as fast as possible, all the while free of worry that a government would investigate and regulate what it was doing.

The global operations of multinational corporations, whether they involved the outsourcing of domestic production to low-wage countries or more purely financial transactions, were critical to their bottom lines. Profits from the foreign operations of U.S. firms represented about 6 percent of total profits in the 1960s but averaged 17 percent from 1990 to 2006. A third of all imports into the United States are from affiliates of U.S. multinationals.

During this explosion of finance, companies we don't usually

THE ORIGIN OF FINANCIAL PROFITS

How have financial companies been able to reap such high profits? They made a portion of their profits from workers (through investments of 401(k) plans, state worker pension funds, etc.) or by creating and selling products to people who had obtained profits in the real economy. Thus what happened was not the creation of new value or wealth but rather a redistribution of wealth as workers' incomes and industrial and service capitalists' profits became targets of potential profit growth by the financial system. Buying companies and loading them up with debt and then reselling the companies—a perfectly legal scam—was behind the wave of "leveraged buyout" acquisitions by private capital. And, as long as prices for companies, stocks, houses, and the like kept going up, it seemed as though people in the financial sector (as well as private investors or speculators) could hardly *not* make a bundle. But the creation of these "profits" was similar to a Ponzi scheme—as long as increasing amounts of money kept coming into the system, driving up prices, it was possible for many investors to get back their investment plus profits. But once the inflow of money dries up a bit—watch out.

think of as "financial," such as insurance corporations, also engaged in many practices similar to those of banks and investment firms. In addition, non-financial companies, such as farm machinery manufacturer John Deere, General Motors, General Electric, and many retailers, made significant income from their financial divisions, so the importance of finance to the economy as a whole grew even larger than indicated by the profits of financial firms.

Many of the financial divisions of corporations, which provided much of their profits before the crisis set in during 2007/2008, are now in trouble because they generated the high profits by the same dubious and dangerous practices followed by strictly financial firms. The rise of the financial system to such prominence in the economy was assisted by an era of deregulation at home and abroad, and sometimes there was no regulation at all.

9. How Did it Happen?

I'd never taken an accounting course, never run a business, never even had savings of my own to manage. I stumbled into a job at Salomon Brothers in 1985 and stumbled out much richer three years later... the whole thing still strikes me as preposterous . . .

I thought I was writing a period piece [in Liar's Poker*] about the 1980s in America. Not for a moment did I suspect that the financial 1980s would last two full decades longer or that the difference in degree between Wall Street and ordinary life would swell into a difference in kind. I expected readers of the future to be outraged that back in 1986, the C.E.O. of Salomon Brothers, John Gutfreund, was paid $3.1 million; I expected them to gape in horror when I reported that one of our traders, Howie Rubin, had moved to Merrill Lynch, where he lost $250 million; I assumed they'd be shocked to learn that a Wall Street C.E.O. had only the vaguest idea of the risks his traders were running. What I didn't expect was that any future reader would look on my experience and say, "How quaint."*

—MICHAEL LEWIS, 2008

"Something for nothing. It never loses its charm," as Michael Lewis puts it. But how did financial firms make money out of money, with no real tangible product and how did the significance of these companies to the economy (along with their profits) grow so rapidly? In the face of huge quantities of money looking for investment opportunities, financial companies expanded dramatically. Here are the most important ways that they did so. They did all of these at the same time, but for clarity, let us look at each one separately.

Financial firms loaned increasing amounts of money to the public (mainly for homes, cars, and credit card debt).

In order to maintain or enhance their standard of living when confronted with stagnating wages, people responded in a number of ways—working longer hours, doing more than one job, and taking on debt. Total household debt in the United States increased from around 40 percent of the GDP in the early 1960s to 100 percent of the GDP in 2007. So, people were not just taking on debt, they were doing so way out of proportion to the growth of the economy. In addition, not only did consumer debt increase relative to the GDP, it also increased relative to people's incomes—doubling from 1975 to 2005, to 127 percent of disposable income. Therefore, people were paying an ever larger portion of their disposable income just to service their debt—more than 14 percent by 2007. Much of this debt stimulated the economy, because people made purchases they wouldn't otherwise have been able to afford. In fact, household spending increased from around 62 percent of the GDP in the early 1980s to around 70 percent in 2007—providing a major underpinning for the economic growth.

Financial firms speculated and developed and peddled increasingly complex financial gimmicks as a primary means of making money.

A profusion of "financial products" (also called "financial instruments") were created and then sold, mainly to wealthy individuals and to institutional investors such as pension funds. Most of these instruments involved what were, in reality, types of bets—some simple, some just a little convoluted, and others highly complex. These "products" were mostly *derivatives*—that is, their value derived from the value of something else, such as a particular interest rate, the value of a currency relative to another currency, a stock market index, the spread in prices of some product over two months, and so forth. Some of these securities were created to offload loans onto others. For example, banks used to keep the mortgage loans they made, and, as the loans were paid off, they would receive the agreed-upon interest and also get back the principal. However, beginning in the 1970s, banks—and then independent mortgage originating companies—began to sell off their loans to others in the so-called secondary market. The next "innovation" was the "securitization" of loans. This involved packaging together loans of various qualities; packages with higher-quality loans (meaning they had a high probability of being paid back) had lower interest rates, and packages with lower-quality loans carried higher interest rates. Mortgages of various qualities were also packaged together, and then these were sometimes "sliced and diced" and rearranged into packages of various sizes and estimated qualities and sold to investors.

THE REAL ECONOMY VERSUS THE PHANTOM ECONOMY

Economists often talk about the "real economy"—where something real is made and sold and services are provided—as opposed to the "financial economy," where paper changes hands for other paper (or these exchanges occur electronically). The real economy is the one in which we dwell as we go about our daily lives, working at a job, buying groceries, and paying electric bills. The "phantom" economy of finance became so large and, to a significant extent, divorced from the real economy that it took on a life of its own. However, the financial system is still linked, sometimes in only indirect and difficult-to-discover ways, to the "real economy." Thus when the financial system begins to falter, it *does* affect the real economy. When the toxic assets on bank balance sheets proved nearly worthless, the banks could no longer lend out mone to consumers and businesses that needed loans to purchase real goods and services, like cars, houses, refrigerators, tool, equipment, and buildings.

No one really understood the value of these complex securities (or "tranches") of different quality mortgages. By 2005, financial companies, which in 1980 got 80 percent of their income from interest on the loans they created, were obtaining only 58 percent of their income from interest, while 42 percent came from fees obtained when they originated or packaged and sold loans. The income-generating machine that developed as mortgage loans were made, packaged as

FINANCIAL INSTRUMENT ALPHABET SOUP

Some types of financial instruments and techniques are familiar to most people—such as stocks, bonds, and certificates of deposit. But a dizzying array of products and strategies is available nowadays. Here are some examples of the major categories (there are many different possibilities within each one):

ABCP — Asset Backed Commercial Paper. Typically 90- to 180-day loans issued by banks and other financial institutions. They are backed by actual assets of the institution. There is also commercial paper that is not backed by any assets, just the promise to pay.

CDO — Collateralized Debt Obligation. Securities backed by a pool of bonds, loans, or other assets. CDOs are divided into "tranches" based on the assumed level of risk, with higher-risk tranches offering higher interest. "Synthetic" CDOs invest in CDSs (see below) or another type of fixed income asset. These are also divided into "tranches." There are also CDOs squared: CDOs backed by CDOs! Mortgages were packaged into CDOs and sold off in various forms to large investors. The packages were designed to have different levels of risk, with the potentially problematic

	ones promising higher interest rates. The spread far and wide of CDOs of dubious quality has greatly contributed to the depth of the current crisis.
CLO	Collateralized Loan Obligation. These are pools of medium to large business loans and sold to owners with different degrees of estimated risk.
COMMERCIAL PAPER	Unlike ABCPs, these are short-term loans from companies that do not have any assets backing them. They are as good as the company's ability to pay.
CDS	Credit Default Swap. Derivatives that take the form of insurance-like contracts, agreements where one party pays a regular premium and in return receives a payment from the second party if some agreed-upon event occurs, frequently the default (or partial payment) of a company's bond. This is a relatively inexpensive way to bet that a company or security will do poorly—much cheaper than "shorting" the company using stock. When you "short" a stock you are betting that the stock price will go down.
DERIVATIVES	Bets derived from one or more underlying assets or conditions. Derivatives allow speculation on the future price or occurrence of just about anything, such as stock prices, interest rates, commodity prices, a national economic index (such as GDP), or the number of sunny days in a given region, without owning any asset at all. Although designed to help hedge against market movements, they have become investments themselves. In 2003, the wealthy investor Warren Buffett called derivatives "financial weapons of mass destruction."

FUTURES Originally used for hedging future prices of agricultural commodities, these are contracts to deliver an asset or settle the contract at a specified future date. Futures were once used mainly by companies that used a product, such as a large bakery using wheat, as a way to control future costs. The futures market became dominated by speculative buying by individuals or hedge funds that had no intention of taking possession of the product. In March of 2008, something like 50 percent of corn in storage was tied up by speculators.

HEDGE FUND Not a financial instrument but rather a business that pools large sums of money from very rich people. Hedge funds have been lightly regulated by governments and have been free to engage in buying and selling nearly any type of financial product, including all of those described here. Managers of these funds, who often earn tens of millions or even a billion dollars in fees, claim that they know how to manage risk so that a high return can be made by investors no matter how well or poorly the overall economy is doing. At their peak in 2008, hedge funds managed about $ 2.5 trillion. The economic crisis has tarnished the image of hedge funds as extraordinary moneymakers, as many have suffered huge losses and some have folded. Some politicians want to regulate these funds, but so far they have not been very successful.

LBO Leveraged Buyout. This occurs when venture capitalists purchase a company and as part of the deal the company takes on debt that is then used to pay fees and other returns to the new owners. Stock in these companies, now loaded with new debt, is then sold to the public. These companies may then close down divisions that are not sufficiently profitable, which will raise the company's short-term profit margin and cause the stock price to rise by signaling to stock buyers that the business is becoming more efficient. Inevitably, mass layoffs of workers accompany leveraged buyouts.

SIV	Structured Investment Vehicle. A technique whereby a bank lends long term to get higher interest rates and borrows short term at lower interest rates by issuing asset-backed commercial paper (ABCP). However, if short-term interest rates increase, a lot of money can be lost in the process. The bank's short-term loans have to be continually paid back, but money from the bank's customers comes back to the bank only in the future. SIVs were mainly "off-balance sheet," meaning they were hidden from view and were not reported as part of financial statements.
SUBPRIME LOANS	Mortgage loans made to people with poor credit histories or low income. Some subprimes were issued without any down payment and required the borrower to pay only the interest for a period. When this period was over, the loan got reset at a higher rate of interest, and people were no longer able make sufficient payments. The ultimate subprime loan was a "ninja," granted with "No verification of Income, Job status or Assets."

collateralized debt obligations (CDOs—for an explanation, see the "Financial Instruments Alphabet Soup" box above), and finally sold off turned into a frenzy of activity. The frenzy of activity was accelerating even as the whole housing pyramid was beginning to topple:

> The Wall Street machine cranked out CDOs full tilt from 2005 to 2007. It was a race against time as accelerating delinquencies ate away at the

> value of mortgage-backed securities that served as collateral for many of the deals. No one was trying to contain the erosion; rather, the players had every incentive to get the securities that backed the deals out of their inventories, so they created as many CDOs as possible.
>
> In just two months (February and March of 2007), one of the world's biggest CDO dealers, Merrill Lynch, sold nearly $29 billion of the securities, 60 percent more than in any previous two-month period, according to data from Thomson Reuters. Goldman Sachs sold $10 billion that March, more than double any previous month. Citigroup sold $9 billion, one-third more than in February, itself a record month.[26]

Most of the financial products were backed by a real asset—not just the promise of a home owner to pay the mortgage but ultimately, if the mortgage wasn't paid, by the house itself. However, many types of financial products were not backed by any asset. Securities were sold that were based on packages of credit card debt, student loans, or corporate loans. These were backed by the promise of the borrower to pay interest and principal on the loan. There were also other "instruments" in which the seller or originator agreed to pay the buyer under certain circumstances—that is, if certain events happened. The number of these types of products was literally endless—you could bet on a change in prices, a difference between prices, or on almost anything. These were sold under an array of acronyms, including SIVs and CDS. Credit default swaps (CDSs), were made legal and not subject to regulation as part of the so-called Commodity Futures Modernization Act, rushed through Congress without debate and signed by President Clinton at the end of 2000.

Some financial products were just bets on such things as whether a particular currency, interest rate, or stock index would go up or down—you could bet either way. Then there was the "carry trade," where large quantities of Japanese yen were borrowed at close to no interest—for years Japan had interest rates close to zero—and invested in countries that had relatively high interest rates such as Iceland, Australia, and New Zealand. This assumed that the relative value of the currencies would remain fairly stable. When the crisis set in during 2008 and the yen appreciated against many other currencies, the carry trade disintegrated. Iceland, a country that based a good part of its "new economy" on its banks borrowing money cheaply abroad and then lending it out inside and outside the country, found itself bankrupt in the fall of 2008.

> "Banks used to want to see you be more conservative," says Daniel O'Connell, chief executive of Vestar Capital Partners, a major private equity firm. "Now they encourage us" to borrow more. The banks are more aggressive because they rarely keep the loans they make. Instead, they sell them to others, who then repackage, or securitize, the loans and sell them to investors as exotic-sounding vehicles such as CLOs, or collateralized-loan obligations. Every week brings announcements of billions of dollars in new CLOs, created by traditional money-management and hedge funds, which then sell them to other investors. In many cases, they may keep some slices of these complicated securities.[27]

Prior to the market crash of 2008, one of the largest single losses taken by a hedge fund occurred in 2006, when a broker at Amaranth Advisors lost a $6 billion bet that the price spread between natural gas prices from one month to another the following spring would move in a certain direction. You can bet on the future prices of commodities and can even bet on the difference in the price of wheat between Kansas City and Chicago. You can construct a derivative that places a bet on literally anything or any combination of things. Mathematicians and physicists, nicknamed "quants," flocked to Wall Street and were paid large sums of money to use their computational skills to devise and value new financial instruments. Many are unemployed today.

Financial firms took on huge amounts of debt in order to make more money on their own "investments."

In other words, when financial firms bought some "investment" they would use $3 or $20 or $30 or more of borrowed money for every dollar they committed of their own—a practice called *leveraging*. Leveraging ratios of over 100 to 1 were common among currency speculators. Highly leveraged bets can be enormously profitable when returns are calculated as a percent of your own money or that of your client. Let's say you borrow $2,000 and use $200 of your own (for a leverage of 10 to 1) and this $2,200 is invested in some way that earns a rate of return of 8 percent in three months—$176 (see Table 3). Of course, you have to pay for the use of the borrowed $2,000, perhaps 5 percent a year. But you only had the money for one-quarter of a year: you'll need to pay interest of $25 (or 0.25 x 0.05 x 2,000), plus the original $2,000, for a total of $2,025. So, you have made $176 – 25 = $151, which works out to a rate of return of 76 percent on the original investment of $200 of your own (or your client's) money, instead of just 8 percent if no leverage was used.

The potential for enormous profits was the reason that so many leveraged transactions occurred. (However, as we will see in the next chapter, when leveraged bets go sour, the losses can also be enormous.) The entire financial system's debt grew faster than any other sector—household, non-financial business, and government debt—from just over 20 percent in 1980 to over 115 percent of the GDP by the end of 2007.

TABLE 3: *Example of Increasing Profits Using Leverage*

Investment:		
Borrowed money	$2,000	Income @ 8% = $160
Own money	$200	Income @ 8% = $16
TOTAL INVESTMENT	$2,200	$176
Cost of borrowed money (for 3 months @ 5% per year)		$25
Net Profit		$151
TOTAL RETURN ON OWN MONEY	$100* ($151/200)	76%

Hedge funds were considered to be "financial engines," even though pension plans, mutual funds, and insurance companies had more assets. This was because these companies traded their holdings rapidly, in 2006 accounting for 30 to 60 percent of all trading in the United States and United Kingdom stock markets. They were the biggest players in some of the more risky types of "investments," such as derivatives and "distressed debt." In the fall of 2008, hedge funds had a bit less than $2 trillion under management, but were leveraged at 3:1 or higher, and so their total "investments" (bets) were around $6 trillion. Many university endowments and pension funds invested in hedge funds and venture capital because of the higher rates of return. During the good times, money flowed freely to the favored few, including the top managers of these funds. Now, college and university endowments have lost so much money that austerity has become the watchword on our campuses, with salary and hiring freezes, layoffs, and mandatory and unpaid leaves. Of course, those hurt most will not be those who made all the money.

EXTENT OF SPECULATION IN STOCKS AND CURRENCIES

In 1975, 19 million stock shares traded daily on the New York Stock Exchange. By 1985, the volume had reached 109 million, and by 2006, 1,600 million shares, with a value of over $60 billion.[28] In June of 2007, 5.2 billion shares were traded, and in October 2008 close to 9 billion were traded in a single day. Even larger is the daily trading on the world currency markets, which has gone from $18 billion a day in 1977 to over $3 trillion a day in 2007. That means that every twenty days, the dollar volume of currency trading equaled the entire world's annual GDP. Currency speculation is especially attractive—you can trade twenty-four hours a day, and it's easy to get in and get out quickly.

The practice of using large leveraging ratios became common once owners of private investment firms sold their companies by "going public"—that is, selling stock shares. A 20- or 30-to-1 (or greater) leverage then made sense because a lot of money and bonuses could be made if the bet went your way. But it would be owners of the company's stock that would take the brunt of any damage if bets went south. In April 2004, the five main large investment banking firms (including Goldman Sachs, whose CEO, Henry Paulson, became the Bush administration's Treasury Secretary in 2006) convinced the Security and Exchange Commission that because their mathematical risk models could predict how much leverage they could safely use, they should be free of the 12-to-1 SEC limit on the amount of debt they could take on. Leverage rose dramatically following this agreement, with Bear Stearns going up to 33 to 1.

The economist Herman Daly has written, "Financial assets have grown by a large multiple of the real economy—paper exchanging for paper is now 20 times greater than exchanges of paper for real commodities."[29] The financial economy, sometimes referred to as a "shadow banking system," greatly overshadows the real economy in which actual physical products are produced and sold and real services provided. This increasingly important sector for generating profits was built on a base of rising levels of debt and the invention of new ways to gamble. It became a highly leveraged giant casino.

Behind every great fortune lies a great crime.
—HONORÉ DE BALZAC

There can be little doubt that outright fraud and shady dealings permeated the financial system. William K. Black, a senior government regulator during the savings and loan debacle of the 1980s, told Bill Moyers that the current financial crisis was driven by fraud. He said that banks knowingly lent money to people they knew could not pay. They then packaged these subprime loans, knowing that they were selling securities of dubious worth. The companies that then sliced and diced the packages and then resold them knew the same thing. So did the rating agencies that gave these bogus financial instruments high-quality ratings. The whole thing was one gigantic fraud, shot through with dishonesty from the beginning. Mr. Black said, "Our [financial] system became a Ponzi scheme. Everybody was buying the pig in the poke. But they were buying the pig in the poke with a pretty pink ribbon, and the pink ribbon said, 'Triple-A.'"

Both political parties helped create the environment that allowed widespread fraud to occur. Clinton favored deregulation as much as Bush. What is more, the people President Obama has put in charge of fixing the mess are, for the most part, the very same persons who perpetrated the fraud. They are doling out money to the same banks and financial companies who were their partners in crime.

Some perpetrators have gone to prison. Several Enron executives spent time in jail, and the most infamous criminal, Bernard Madoff (a former Nasdaq stock exchange official), created a Ponzi scheme in which a variety of wealthy people were defrauded of an estimated $50 billion), and will probably die in prison. Many more are yet to be caught, although most will escape the justice system. When so much money is at stake and changing hands rapidly, fortunes seem to appear out of thin air. Those in Congress who pushed deregulation of financial institutions and agencies such as Moody's that rated the quality of investments sold whatever ethics they had for hard cash. The institutions that created subprime mortgages and peddled them to people who were clearly not going to be able to keep up payments are also to blame.

However, the underlying problem was not corruption, lax oversight, or deregulation—these are only symptoms of a sick economy and society—but rather an economic system that was responding to stagnation of the *real* economy. In a society that prays to the money gods, corruption is unavoidable after the discovery of magical new ways to turn money into more money without producing anything.[30]

The financial companies encouraged deregulation and often engaged in fraud or at the least lax business practices.

There is no doubt that the explosive growth of the financial system was assisted by deregulation in the 1990s and 2000s, the lack of reg-

> [Hedge fund trader Steve] Eisman knew that subprime lenders could be scumbags. What he underestimated was the total unabashed complicity of the upper class of American capitalism. . . . He couldn't figure out exactly how the rating agencies justified turning BBB loans into AAA-rated bonds. "I didn't understand how they were turning all this garbage into gold," he says. . . . He called Standard & Poor's and asked what would happen to default rates if real estate prices fell. The man at S & P couldn't say; its model for home prices had no ability to accept a negative number. "They were just assuming home prices would keep going up," Eisman says.
>
> —MICHAEL LEWIS

ulation of new types of practices and gambling schemes (financial instruments), fraud on the part of the peddlers of the new schemes, and extremely lax business practices. The lobbying efforts of the financial giants were based upon the ideology of neoliberalism, which had become accepted in much of the economics profession—get the government out of the way and let the "free" market work its wonders.

One "reform" of the financial system was the misleadingly titled 1999 Financial Services Modernization Act, which, among other provisions, repealed the Glass-Steagall Act. The purpose of the Glass-Steagall Act, passed during the Great Depression, was meant to prevent some of the abuses that have made the current crisis so severe. The act separated investment banks (which help sell bonds and stocks) from commercial banks (which take in deposits and lend money for buying homes and other purposes). With so much money to be made, however, commercial banks in 1991 wanted to get into the more profitable business of underwriting the issuing of stock. At the same time, brokerage firms wanted to "reform" the law so they could sell stocks more easily to a large number of commercial bank customers. Other changes included the SEC rule that allowed financial firms to decide how much leverage to use, based on their mathematical risk models.

The new mortgage-based bonds were complex, and purchasers relied on rating agencies such as Standard & Poor's and Moody's to assign a relative credit risk to each. The housing boom generated considerable business for the rating companies. These firms were paid by the bond issuer to rate their bonds, inviting conflicts of interest. Within seven years, Moody's income from rating the various mortgage and consumer loan products went from $200 to $900 million.

When a bond was rated below what the issuer wanted, complaints frequently got the rating companies to increase the rating. Answering an internal management survey as things were starting to fall apart in 2007, a managing director of Moody's wrote: "These errors make us look either incompetent at credit analysis or like we sold our soul to the devil for revenue, or a little bit of both."[31]

10. The Explosion of Debt

No, it's not Las Vegas or Atlantic City. It's the U.S. financial system. The volume of transactions has boomed far beyond anything needed to support the economy. Borrowing—politely called leverage—is getting out of hand. And futures enable people to play the market without owning a share of stock. The result: the system is tilting from investment to speculation.

—*BUSINESS WEEK*, September 16, 1985

The explosion of debt was directly related to, and encouraged by, the growth of the importance of financial institutions in the economy. High levels of debt (leverage) were used to enhance the profit-making potential of various bets. One of the ways to make money with money is to lend it out, sell the loan and pocket the fees, and continue making loans. Now, none of this would work if there were no borrowing. So, credit was made easier to come by. There was a time when, if you didn't receive multiple credit card offers through the mail every week, you wondered what was wrong. Lenders hustled car loans, credit cards, house loans, and business loans to every possible borrower. In the mid-1960s, debt began to grow more rapidly than the economy—especially in certain sectors—and in the mid-1980s, this growth of debt accelerated. Then, in the mid-1990s, household and financial institution debt started to enter the stratosphere. Household debt and financial business debt were the two sectors that increased the most dramatically—with household debt climbing by 2007 to 100 percent of the GDP and financial business debt increasing sevenfold as a percent of the GDP, reaching 116 percent in 2007. Non-financial business debt as a percent of the economy increased as well, but at a much slower pace than household debt and financial business debt. Government debt (local, state, and federal) increased through the mid-1990s and then decreased somewhat.

By 2007, all U.S. debt, including household, business, and government (local, state, and federal), was approximately 350 percent of the GDP.[32] When money is borrowed and spent, the economy is stimulated, and this can help a mature capitalist economy counteract its tendency to grow slowly. Private sector deficit spending can continue as long as people and corporations have enough income to service their debts. (The U.S. government can actually print more money, if needed.) However, just as a household's rent or mortgage payments cannot keep growing faster than the household's income, so too the amount of debt in the economy cannot forever grow faster than the underlying economy, or GDP, because the growth of the economy determines the capacity of debtors to repay the loans. And the higher the amount of debt relative to the GDP, the more fragile the system becomes. A major downturn will limit the ability of people and companies to continue paying their high debts—as is happening right now. It has been the increased debt and the buying it allowed that has kept the economy from growing even more slowly than it has over the last quarter-century. So now we have an economy that apparently cannot live without more and more debt, and, at the same time, we have an economic crisis in which most people and corporations will probably not be able to pay back any new debt they obtain (assuming they are even able to get new loans). This does not bode well for economic growth in the coming years.

Debt-financed consumer spending allowed U.S. consumers to buy large quantities of goods and services produced abroad, often by U.S. multinationals outsourcing work previously done in the home country. The rapid growth of imports, coupled with the sluggish growth of exports, contributed greatly to another source of economic fragility—people in the United States spent more money for things produced in foreign countries than foreigners spent for what was produced here. One thing that has helped to strengthen the world economic and political position of the United States over the last sixty years is that the dollar is the major currency accepted in international transactions. Almost every purchase of something that originates abroad requires that dollars be supplied to pay for it. For example, oil prices are quoted, and settled when sold, in dollars. In this way, dollars travel outside the United States. But because of the imbalance, with so much more bought from abroad than sold there from the United States, there is an oversupply of dollars in the world relative to foreign currencies. But if dollars stay abroad and don't return (as purchases of government bonds, stocks, or property) a currency crisis will develop. In 2007, the huge disparity

FIGURE 1: *Debt as a Percent of GDP*

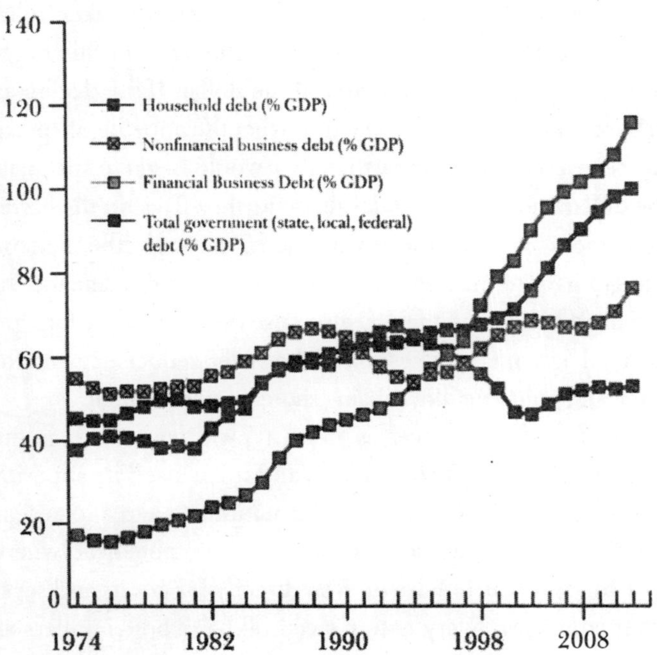

with the rest of the world—with so much more consumed in the United States from abroad than the country exports—amounted to $2 billion per day, 365 days a year, and over the last four years has represented more than 5 percent of each year's GDP.

Under typical circumstances, a nation with a large trade deficit will find its currency depreciated, that is, exchanging for less and less foreign currency. As with anything else, when supply greatly exceeds demand, prices fall. In this case, the price is the exchange rate of the dollar with euros, yen, and other foreign monies. The dollar has gone through a number of cycles, increasing in value relative to other currencies at certain times (the early 1980s and late 1990s) only to then depreciate significantly. If the exchange value of the dollar were to fall dramatically, this would make imports to the United States more expensive (for example, more dollars would have to be paid for a certain number of yen than before), and by raising the price of consumer goods that would increase inflation in the United States. If the foreign goods and services did not have acceptable substitutes, U.S. consumers might continue buying them at the higher prices and cut back on things produced here, leading to unemployment. A weaker dollar would also encourage foreigners to buy U.S. exports, but this might not be enough to stop the devaluation of the dollar. If the decline in the dollar's exchange value fell enough to whet the appetite of speculators who believed it might fall further, they would begin to speculate against the dollar and this would devalue it further. To stop the harmful consequences of this, the government, through the Federal Reserve, might have to push interest rates up to raise the demand for U.S. government bonds and thereby also raise the demand by foreigners for dollars. High interest rates would, however, reduce demand for houses, cars, and construction, causing more unemployment.

The United States, however, is not a typical country. It is the world's most powerful capitalist nation, and it has used its superior economic and military power to get other nations to agree to accept the U.S. dollar as a leading global currency, acceptable everywhere in exchange for other currencies or even directly for goods and services in other countries. Every nation's central bank holds dollars as a reserve currency, to be used in emergencies. If the yen begins to depreciate in value, the Japanese central bank can use its dollar reserves to buy yen and keep the yen exchange rate stable. What is more, the long-term political stability and economic prowess of the United States makes the bonds issued by the U.S. government among the safest in the world. The federal government has never defaulted on its bonds. And until recently, stocks in U.S. corporations and real estate in large U.S. cities seemed to foreigners to be good investments. So, much of the excess supply of dollars in the world either stayed in foreign central banks or flowed back to the United States as U.S. government bonds, corporate stocks, and real estate were bought by foreign persons, businesses, and governments. No other country has this luxury. After all, what would one do with large and increasing amounts of Icelandic kronas, Mexican pesos, or Ghanian cedis? These currencies are worthless for purchasing merchandise outside the issuing country. The fact that the United States can run up large international deficits without causing its currency to depreciate in value as much as it should means that interest rates in the United States can be lower than they would otherwise be. Therefore, foreigners in effect helped subsidize the housing boom and all other spending that relied on borrowing.

The willingness of foreign interests to purchase U.S. government bonds, notes, and bills conferred another advantage upon the economy. Most government bonds are sold at auctions; the potential buyers bid on them. Suppose a $100, five-year Treasury note is for sale and it pays an annual rate of 2 percent. If the highest bid is $90, the buyer gets the bond for $90 and will receive $100 when the bond matures in five years plus the promised annual $2 interest. Thus, after 5 years the person gets $20 ($10 from interest and $10 because of the low purchase price) for an investment of $90, or an average annual rate of about 4.4 percent. For short-term U.S. government notes, maturing in a year or less, there is no interest rate promised and interest received is therefore based on the difference between the purchase price and the face value that the government promises to repay when the note is due. Notice that the effective interest will be higher (and the burden on the government higher since it has to pay the interest) the lower the price is at which the bond initially sells. As Chinese, Japanese, and other central banks and governments, as well as businesses and individuals (all told, foreign individuals, banks, and governments hold as much as half of the privately held debt of the United States government), boosted the demand for these bonds, their prices remained higher and their interest rates lower than they would otherwise have been. If we remember that the U.S. government issues bonds in the first place to pay for its spending in excess of its tax revenues, we see that the government could finance spending well in excess of taxes, stimulating the economy to a greater extent than it otherwise could have (and without raising taxes), because it would not incur huge interest obligations.

Readers should be able to figure out at this point what would happen if the U.S. government's profligate ways someday spook foreigners into considering that their money invested in assets in the United States might be safer somewhere else. There are already rumblings that this could well happen. Just put the above analysis in reverse.

The debt and credit binge of the past few years worked out pretty well for the wealthy. The financial boom was, in fact, a continuation of the class war against workers. As they say, "The proof is in the pudding." Despite sometimes valiant efforts by some unions and other progressive organizations, the entire system of laws, regulations, and taxes was arranged by the wealthy in order to help them make more and more money out of the growth of the financial system they promoted. The environment created by the increasing role of finance (financialization) of the economy—the huge increases in debt, the unparalleled number of ways to speculate and the actual amount of betting, the government stepping in when needed to clean up a mess here or there, the workings of the Federal Reserve keeping interest rates low so as to promote the increasing prices of assets, the decrease in taxes on the rich (via the unfounded assumption that they would invest more in the real economy) and so on—all worked to distribute more of economic wealth away from workers and toward producing record profits for the wealthy. Business profits, which had reached their nadir of less than 5 percent of the GDP in the mid-1980s, rebounded rapidly so that by 2006 profits were over 11 percent of the GDP. Between 1974 and 2004, the average after-tax income of the wealthiest 1 percent of the population increased by 176 percent, or by $553,800. On the other hand, the poorest 20 percent of the population saw their average after-tax income increase by only 6 percent—$800—during the same period. The change of income distribution over time has been pretty dramatic. In 2006, the top 10 percent received close to 50 percent of all income in the United States, up from about 33 to 35 percent for most of the period from 1940 to the early 1980s (Figure 2). Wealth distribution also changed greatly during this period, and by 2004, the top 1 percent owned about one-third of all the net worth (wealth minus debts) in the United States, with the top 20 percent controlling 85 percent of the net worth (Table 4). At the same time, the bottom 80 percent of the people had only 15 percent of the total national net worth.[33]

FIGURE 2: *Income Share of the Top Ten Percent in the United States, 1917–2006*

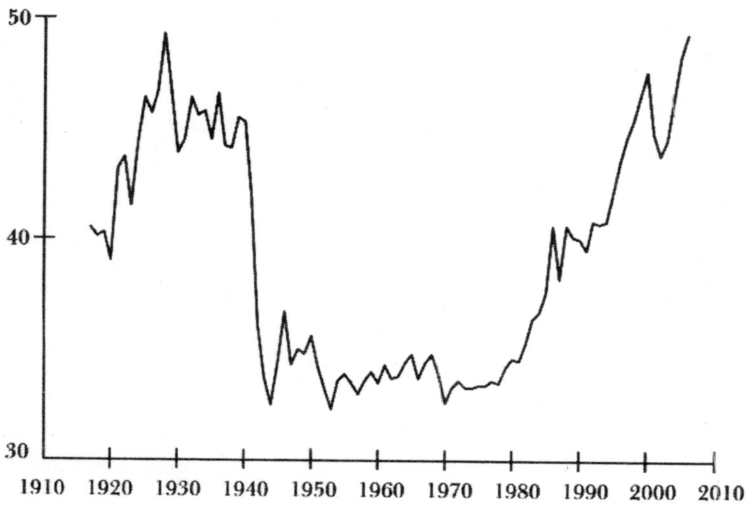

Source: Piketty and Saez (2003), series updated to 2006. Income is defined as market income including capital gains. In 2006, top decile includes all families with more than $104,700 of annual income.

TABLE 4: *Household Distribution of Net Worth in the United States (2001)*

Percent of Families	Percent of Net Worth
Top 1%	33.4%
Top 5%	59.2%
Top 10%	71.5%
Top 20%	84.4%
Bottom 80%	15.5%
Bottom 40%	0.3%

Source: Changes in Household Wealth in the 1980s and 1990s in the U.S., in Edward N. Wolff, ed. 2006. International Perspectives on Household Wealth (Elgar Publishing Ltd.)

The growth of inequality in wealth and income for the last quarter-century wasn't just an accident. Everything was rigged to encourage it to happen. And the wealthy few made out like bandits (and some actually *were* bandits), while the vast majority of people fell into deep debt in order to keep up or get ahead. There was a great wealth shift to the already wealthy while the social safety nets were being made less secure.

In the 1980s, President Ronald Reagan's advisors argued that the problem with the economy was that the rich weren't rich enough, and if given more money, they would invest it, helping to create jobs. They also maintained that the poor weren't poor enough. Overly generous social welfare programs encouraged the poor to collect welfare rather than work. This way of thinking led to policies that helped to start a huge redistribution of income and wealth from the bottom to the top. However, the decreased share of the economic pie going to workers and the ever-increasing share going to the wealthy over the last quarter-century has made it more difficult to sustain capitalism on an even keel over the long haul. There was so much money in the hands of the wealthy that they had no productive way to use it. If a greater share had been in the hands of workers, this money would have been spent on commodities of all kinds, generating output and employment without such a massive accumulation of household debt.

11. The Great Unraveling

The current financial debacle is really not a "liquidity" crisis as it is often euphemistically called. It is a crisis of overgrowth of financial assets relative to growth of real wealth—pretty much the opposite of too little liquidity.

—HERMAN DALY, 2008

Many economists thought that by the beginning of the 1990s the economy had become more resistant to shocks than in the past. Things seemed to return to normal reasonably quickly following a crisis. The recoveries in the late 1990s from the failure of the Long-Term Capital Management hedge fund and the Asian financial crisis were viewed as proof of this. The newfangled financial "instruments," which appeared to spread risk more widely, were presumed to make a financial crash or severe recession less likely. This "new economy" was believed to behave according to new rules—with asset prices going up forever, as if physicists had found some way to repeal the law of gravity. In reality, however, a fragile situation had developed, characterized by a) a huge amount of debt permeating the entire system; b) an unprecedented degree of highly leveraged pure speculation relying on ever-increasing prices; c) a redistribution of income and wealth upward, resulting in difficult economic conditions for the mass of people; d) more immediate and direct economic connections—financial and trade—among nations around the globe; and e) a huge and continuing U.S. negative trade balance with the rest of the world.

A deep crisis, the "big one," was postponed time and again, through mainly monetary means. First, U.S. markets were flooded with money and supported by low interest rates maintained in the aftermath of the Asian financial crisis of the late 1990s, which helped create the tech stock bubble. And then, after that bubble burst, low interest rates and easily available money led to the rapid rise in housing prices. The attempted remedies for dealing with one crisis led inexorably to the next one. While mainstream economists and the media were in a competition to see which could heap the most praise on the "new economy" and the miracle-working "oracle," Federal Reserve chairman Greenspan, leftists who actually studied the workings of the economy understood that there was a serious problem with mature capitalism. Writing about the bailing out of the system following each crisis, Harry Magdoff and Paul Sweezy said this in 1988:

> But, you may ask, won't the powers that be step into the breach again and abort the crisis before it gets a chance to run its course? Yes, certainly. That, by now, is standard operating procedure, and it cannot be excluded that it will succeed in the same ambiguous sense that it did after the 1987 stock market crash. If so, we will have the whole process to go through again on a more elevated and more precarious level. But sooner or later, next time or further down the road, it will not succeed....We will then be in a new situation as unprecedented as the conditions from which it will have emerged.[34]

Now, twenty-one years later, we are facing precisely the unprecedented situation referred to—caused by nipping crisis after crisis in the bud without solving the underlying problem of the growth of finance as a response to stagnation. Instead of "solving" the system's problem, the responses only served to delay the day of reckoning. And because the structural problems continued to grow, delaying the "correction" only increased the severity of the eventual downfall. The developing bubble in the housing market in the early to mid-2000s was clear for all to see—if they looked. Starting in 2001, home prices increased dramatically, out of all relation to other indices, including the costs of building houses (see Figure 3).[35]

Very low interest rates, lax lending practices, the packaging and selling of mortgages (so that whether the mortgage was actually paid didn't matter to the company that originated the mortgage) spurred the growth of the housing bubble. Speculation also played an important part, as people purchased homes or condominium units only to sell them weeks or months later. This contributed to the rise of a popular new phrase: "flipping houses." (One stockbroker in New York commented on a news show that he first knew something was wrong when his dentist told him that he owned five condos in Florida.) The 1997 tax change that permitted people who had occupied their homes for two years to exclude up to $500,000 of gain when they sold their house also increased speculation, as some people sold their homes and purchased others only to resell them after two years and go through another cycle.

FIGURE 3: *Inflation-adjusted Index of U.S. Home Prices and Building Costs (1979 = 100), Interest Rates, and Population*

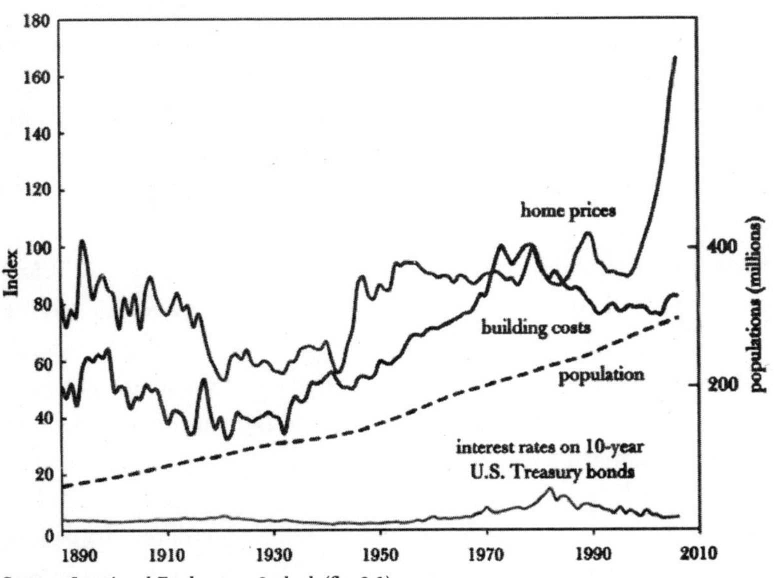

Source: *Irrational Exuberance*, 2nd ed. (fig. 2.1)

In the summer of 2007 two hedge funds run by the investment bank Bear Stearns failed. It soon became clear that there were a lot of packages of "toxic waste"—mortgages that were not paying what had been promised—in the financial system and held by pension funds and other large institutions in the United States and abroad. Things quickly went from bad to worse, as the housing bubble burst and home prices started to decline. The subprime mortgages—which really should be called high-cost mortgages because of the extra fees and interest charged—were structured in such a way that a low-income family might be able to pay the mortgage until it reset a year or so later at a higher interest rate. Some mortgages allowed payment of interest-only at the beginning, with ballooning payments when higher interest *and* principal needed to be paid. As home values decreased, it was estimated in the fall of 2008 that more was owed on some twelve million homes than the homes were actually worth. Both poor and not so poor people were unable to make their mortgage payments, and home prices continued to fall. At this point, foreclosures began in earnest.

The value of the packaged mortgages securities started to fall even more, setting off problems for institutions owning these financial instruments. In 2005 and 2006, no United States banks failed. Then in 2007 three banks failed, and in 2008 bank failures accelerated—twenty-five were taken over by the Federal Deposit Insurance Corporation. Bank failures continued at an even faster pace in 2009, with seventy-two failing by early August. By the end of 2008, over two million homes entered foreclosure proceedings and close to 7 percent of all mortgages were not keeping up with payments. Problems started to develop with commercial real estate, as well as consumer credit card debt and products based on these debts. As housing prices fell and the crisis in the financial system got under way, consumers began to spend less money and credit froze. The near-demise of the financial sector and the inability of businesses to borrow money meant that the real economy started to spiral downward. The U.S. economy entered a recession in December of 2007. Growth slowed considerably, and in the first twelve months of the recession, about 2.5 million people lost their jobs, about one-half million in each of November and December

2008. Job loss continues in 2009, with more than a half million jobs lost each month of the first quarter. Close to seven million jobs have been lost since the start of the crisis. That doesn't account for the approximately 1.5 million extra jobs that should have been created each year just to keep up with the number of people coming of age and wanting to enter the labor force, minus those leaving because of retirement. Although the official jobless rate in August 2009 stood at 9.4%, including part time workers that want full time jobs and people who have given up looking for work (and therefore aren't considered unemployed) brings the total to 19%—or approximately 30 million people. As we write this book, some economists are pointing to "green shoots" of positive news that indicates that the worst might be over. However, there is no end to the misery in sight, not here in the United States or in any country in the world. It will certainly take a long time to replace all the jobs lost in the current crisis. As we noted above, after the last recession, ending in 2001, it took four years to replace the jobs lost in the downturn and some states never did. This time around, it is difficult to see how states like Michigan, ravaged by the collapse of Chrysler and General Motors, will ever recover.

12. The Government to the Rescue?

At first I thought we could deal with this_deal with the problem one issue at a time. We made the decision on Fannie and Freddie because there was systemic risk to our mortgage markets. And then obviously AIG came along, and Lehman came along and it was_it declared bankruptcy; then AIG came along and it_the house of cards was much bigger, beyond_started to stretch beyond just Wall Street, in the sense of the effects of failure. And so when one card started to go, we were worried about the whole deck going down.

—PRESIDENT G. W. BUSH, September 20, 2008

Before we look at attempts by the government to end the crisis, we must note two things. First, while public officials will claim that what they are doing is motivated by concern for the people, reality suggests otherwise. The financial titans who triggered this mess have given large sums of money to the elected officials charged with the cleanup and recovery. They are also deeply and directly involved in the government, as both appointed officers and advisors. In an interview with the former chief economist at the International Monetary Fund, journalist Bill Moyers said this:

> Geithner [current Treasury Secretary Timothy Geithner] has hired as his chief-of-staff, the lobbyist from Goldman Sachs. The new deputy sec-

retary of state was, until last year, a CEO of Citigroup. Another CFO from Citigroup is now assistant to the president, and deputy national security advisor for International Economic Affairs. And one of his deputies also came from Citigroup. One new member of the president's Economic Recovery Advisory Board comes from UBS, which is being investigated for helping rich clients evade taxes.[36]

THE POWER OF FINANCIAL INTERESTS

In his article "The Quiet Coup" in the May 2009 issue of *The Atlantic Monthly*, Simon Johnson makes a persuasive argument that there has been a "reemergence of an American financial oligarchy." Whether or not the group of people leading the financial sector of the United States economy is a true oligarchy, it is beyond debate that they wield extraordinary power and influence. Using large contributions to politicians and mobilizing a sizable group of lobbyists they have been able to make sure that laws and regulations are enacted that they consider are in their best interests. As Joseph Stiglitz, winner of the Bank of Sweden's Nobel Memorial Prize in Economic Sciences, has put it: "America has expanded its corporate safety net in unprecedented ways, from commercial banks to investment banks, then to insurance and now to cars, with no end in sight. In truth ... this is ... an extension of long-standing corporate welfarism. The rich and powerful turn to the government to help them whenever they can, while needy individuals get little social protection."

Although the legal and regulatory framework they created through the financial sector's influence in Congress and the regulatory agencies has contributed to our economic troubles, it is not the underlying cause of the current economic crisis.

It would be logical to expect that the power of the top financial interests would have diminished considerably because of their contribution to the mess we now face and the hundreds of billions of dollars used by the federal government to bail out the financial system. But it turns out that they are still able to more-or-less get their way—with an occasional symbolic slap on the wrist. It now appears that, despite all the talk about how much damage was caused by greed of financial interests, little will actually change in the basic structure of the financial system. As Stiglitz explains regarding the banks, "Another problem with America's too-big-to-fail, too-big-to-be-restructured banks . . . [is that] they are too politically powerful. Their lobbying efforts worked well, first to deregulate and then to have taxpayers pay for the cleanup. Their hope is that it will work once again to keep them free to do as they please, regardless of the risks for taxpayers and the economy."

Just a few examples should give some indication of the power of financial interests:

- The so-called Financial Services Modernization Act passed late in 1999 did away with the Depression-era Glass-Steagall Act, which separated investment banks from commercial banks and helped to limit the growing power and concentration of the financial industry.

- In 2000, the Commodity Futures Modernization Act went through both houses of Congress without debate shortly before the Christmas holiday and was quickly signed into law by President Clinton. It was designed to prohibit the regulation or oversight of derivatives such as credit default swaps (CDSs).

- The Homeland Investment Act of 2004 was designed to give a very low tax to corporations that brought profits earned abroad into the United States. The corporations (financial as well as non-financial) claimed that they would invest their repatriated profits and thereby stimulate the economy. However, it turns out that almost all the repatriated funds were either given out in dividends to bond holders or used to buy back stock, helping to increase the value of the remaining stock.

- Also in 2004, lobbying by top bankers caused the Securities and Exchange Commission to do away with guidelines and allow banks to decide how much debt to take on (leverage) when making their "bets." As a result, the amount of leverage on their "investments" soared.

- When much of the financial industry went bust or was in deep trouble, there were a number of alternative ways for the government to react. For example, a logical way to proceed with the large bankrupt banks would have been to take them over and break them up, converting them into institutions that were *not* "too large to fail." But stock and bond holders could have lost a lot of money that way, and the industry and its allies fought against the threat they referred to as "nationalization," even though banks would have been in government hands only temporarily. Government officials who had previously worked in finance or were personally close to people in the industry devised the bailout of the financial industry. Beginning in the fall of 2008 with the "$700 billion bailout," every step of the way has been engineered to ensure the continuation of the industry in more-or-less its previous form, its power undiminished. To date, financial institutions have beaten back efforts to limit their ability to function as they wish and to maintain their prominence in the economy. They may, at least for a while, be forced to accept limited oversight of hedge funds and complex derivatives.

- An example from 2009 is the financial interests working hard and successfully to make sure that a key provision was not included in the Helping Families Save Their Homes Act. This would have allowed judges in bankruptcy proceedings to lower the amount of money owed on a person's home mortgage. As it now stands, a judge can order a reduced amount to be paid on a second home or a yacht but not on one's primary (or only) residence.

The former Treasury Secretary, Henry Paulson, was formerly the chairman and CEO of Goldman Sachs, one of Wall Street's most important investment banks. While there, he was a champion of the deregulation of financial markets—including ending the Securities and Exchange Commission rules that limited the leveraging of debt—that has helped cause so much economic chaos. When some of the nation's top bankers appeared before Congress in February of 2009, they were handled with kid gloves. The economist interviewed by Mr. Moyers, Simon Johnson, told him, "I called up one of my friends on Capitol Hill after that testimony, and that session. I said, 'What happened? This was your moment. Why did they pull their punches like that?' And my friend said, 'They, the Committee members, know the bankers too well.'" Timothy Geithner himself was formerly president of the New York Federal Reserve Bank, and while there he fought against financial regulation and, as recent accounts have noted, was extraordinarily cozy with the corporate executives whose companies he is now to bring to heel. All in all, there is no reason to believe that, absent mass protests, the architects of government economic policies will keep the working-class majority uppermost in their minds.

In a recent article in *The Atlantic Monthly*, Mr. Johnson goes even further and states that the financiers of the United States have staged a "quiet coup" and taken over the federal government. He uses his experiences as the chief economist of the IMF to buttress his claim. Usually the IMF is called in to help straighten out an economic mess in an "emerging economy." It is worth quoting him at length:

> Emerging-market governments and their private-sector allies commonly form a tight-knit—and, most of the time, genteel—oligarchy, running the country rather like a profit-seeking company in which they are the controlling shareholders. When a country like Indonesia or South Korea or Russia grows, so do the ambitions of its captains of industry. As masters of their mini-universe, these people make some investments that clearly benefit the broader economy, but they also start making bigger and riskier bets. They reckon—correctly, in most cases—that their political connections will allow them to push onto the government any substantial problems that arise....
>
> But inevitably, emerging-market oligarchs get carried away; they waste money and build massive business empires on a mountain of debt. Local banks, sometimes pressured by the government, become too willing to extend credit to the elite and to those who depend on them. Overborrowing always ends badly, whether for an individual, a

company, or a country. Sooner or later, credit conditions become tighter and no one will lend you money on anything close to affordable terms.

The downward spiral that follows is remarkably steep. Enormous companies teeter on the brink of default, and the local banks that have lent to them collapse. Yesterday's "public-private partnerships" are relabeled "crony capitalism." With credit unavailable, economic paralysis ensues, and conditions just get worse and worse. The government is forced to draw down its foreign-currency reserves to pay for imports, service debt, and cover private losses. But these reserves will eventually run out. If the country cannot right itself before that happens, it will default on its sovereign debt and become an economic pariah. The government, in its race to stop the bleeding, will typically need to wipe out some of the national champions—now hemorrhaging cash—and usually restructure a banking system that's gone badly out of balance. It will, in other words, need to squeeze at least some of its oligarchs.

Squeezing the oligarchs, though, is seldom the strategy of choice among emerging-market governments. Quite the contrary: at the outset of the crisis, the oligarchs are usually among the first to get extra help from the government, such as preferential access to foreign currency, or maybe a nice tax break, or . . . the assumption of private debt obligations by the government. Under duress, generosity toward old friends takes many innovative forms. Meanwhile, needing to squeeze someone, most emerging-market governments look first to ordinary working folk—at least until the riots grow too large.[37]

If this sounds familiar, Johnson tells us it should. The tremendous growth of the financial sector has made the captains of Wall Street just like the Russian oligarchs, overseers of businesses too big to fail and so deeply intertwined with the political elite that it has come to be public policy that what is good for Wall Street is good for the country. Nothing could be further from the truth, but as long as it is thought to be true by those in power, the less likely it will be that government policies will address what is really wrong with the economy.

It is also necessary to understand that nearly all of those formulating, legislating, and administering bailouts and stimulus packages not so long ago believed that what is happening now in the United States and nearly every country in the world could not happen. They championed neoliberalism, believing that markets were self-regulating and that all of the participants were rational and therefore acted rationally. *Why should anyone now believe that these people know what they are doing?* One of President Obama's top economic advisors is the previously mentioned Lawrence Summers. The advice he gave as a highly paid consultant to Lithuania and Russia was that they should speed up their transition from socialism to capitalism by embracing neoliberalism as fast as they were able. The results were catastrophic. Mass economic hardship caused the suicide rate in Lithuania to double, and Russia became the first advanced industrial nation in history to endure a sharp decline in life expectancies. This is also the same person who earned over $5 million working for one of the largest hedge funds and speaking to banks such as Citigroup for the two years before joining the Obama administration. Is Mr. Summers now going to tell us how to reverse the crisis in which we now find ourselves? Don't hold your breath. It is remarkable that Obama, for all his professed liberalism, has not called on those few mainstream economists who do have a better grasp of what is happening and what needs to be done (note that we say "better" and not "best"—no orthodox economists have admitted or will ever admit the truth—that the system itself is rotten and needs to be replaced). Nobel laureates Paul Krugman and Joseph Stiglitz, along with iconoclasts like Nouriel Roubini, could much better advise the government than the "experts" now on board, but apparently they are too far left to be considered as advisors.

Credit froze once the housing bubble began to burst, and it became apparent that the securitized mortgages and all the other complex financial instruments that were held by investment banks, brokerages, commercial banks, hedge funds, pension funds, local and state governments and school districts in all corners of the United States were of dubious value. Financial institutions knew that they might be insolvent (their assets, now mainly "toxic," would not be high enough to cover their liabilities), and if this were so, it would be foolish to loan money. What borrowers could be trusted? Cold, hard cash was what was needed. Consumers, strapped with debts and facing foreclosures on their homes, could not take on more debt. The credit collapse created enormous uncertainty for businesses, and they responded rationally by refusing to spend their money. They put plans to expand or replace capital (buildings, machines, and so forth) on hold. They couldn't even secure the short-term loans they always counted on to meet immediate costs. This inability to borrow began to threaten their solvency as well.

With investment banks and the world's largest insurer (AIG) about to fail, the government had to take action. The global intertwining of financial markets, their continued ties to the "real" economy, and the almost incomprehensible size of their assets—many trillions of dollars—meant that failures could plunge economies into depressions and political turmoil not seen since the 1930s. To the powers that be, this was unthinkable. So even that champion of unregulated markets, President George W. Bush, knew that something had to be done.

Federal government economic policy is of two types: monetary and fiscal.[38] The former is the province of the Federal Reserve; the latter is controlled by Congress and the president. Monetary policy aims to influence the availability of credit, and it has a wide variety of tools at its disposal. The Federal Reserve consists of twelve Federal Reserve banks located around the country. The most important is in New York City, the nation's financial capital. The Federal Reserve system is managed by the seven-member Board of Governors, headed by the Chairman of the Board of Governors (Ben Bernanke is the current chairman). The Board, along with the officers of the twelve Federal Reserve banks, sets the nation's monetary policy. During the current crisis, Bernanke has been coordinating policies with the Secretary of the Treasury, currently Timothy Geithner.

Whereas monetary policy affects spending, production, and employment indirectly by first changing the availability of credit, fiscal policy attempts to influence these economic flows directly by altering the federal government's budgets. The budget consists of government spending (including payments on past debt), tax receipts, and new debt (if tax revenues are less than the amount of spending, the government must borrow the difference by issuing and selling bonds). Fiscal policy, then, includes raising or lowering taxes, increasing or decreasing spending, and taking on or paying off debt. Since past ups and downs in the economy have been dealt with successfully (from the point of view of the economic elite) by the Federal Reserve, the government assumed that Fed chairman Ben Bernanke could take care of things. The Fed began with its tried and true measures, but when these did not work, Bernanke expanded the Fed's tool kit to an unprecedented degree, doing things that have never been done before. So far, the Fed has:

- *Pushed interest rates to near zero.* The Fed did this mainly by lowering to near zero the rate at which banks lend money to another overnight and for very short periods of time. These loans had been among the safest a bank could make, yet credit dried up to such an extent that banks did not trust one another to make what were once routine loans. The Fed also initiated programs to encourage banks to borrow directly from it, at what is called the "discount window." Ordinarily, a bank that borrowed from the Fed had to put up high-grade, short-term commercial paper as collateral. The Fed began to take lesser quality paper and extend the loan period. The New York Federal Reserve Bank provided funding for Morgan Stanley's purchase of Bear Stearns. Morgan Stanley put up assets as collateral, but the Fed agreed to assume some of the losses if these assets proved to be worthless. The New York Fed also agreed to lend large sums of money to the federally regulated—and now nationalized—mortgage guarantee companies Freddie Mac and Fannie Mae and to troubled companies such as American International Group (AIG), the world's largest insurance company.

- *Established a number of special lending facilities in an attempt to put more liquidity (money) into the financial system.* In the Term Securities Lending Facility (March 11, 2008), the Fed allows the large banks and securities firms that traditionally deal directly with the Federal Reserve banks to obtain very low-risk federal government Treasury securities and in return give the government the higher-risk assets—such as mortgage-backed securities—that these institutions hold. Then the Treasury securities can be sold for cash, giving these institutions money to lend out. The Primary Dealer Credit Facility (March 16, 2008) allows the Fed to lend money directly to these financial organizations, which is the first time in its history the Fed has permitted this. Another entity was set up to provide funds to money market funds after the biggest one, Reserve Primary Fund, ran into such trouble that it could only pay depositors less than a dollar for each dollar deposited. A fourth agency, the Commercial Paper Funding Facility, was opened on October 7, 2008, to purchase commercial paper, a basic source of corporate financing that banks would no longer buy. Yet another of its new lending programs, the Term Asset-Backed Securities Lending Facility (TALF), was given birth on November 25, 2008, to provide money in exchange for still other troubled assets such as consumer loans.

- *Provided central banks around the world with hundreds of billions of dollars through swaps of dollars for foreign currency.* Other countries need dollars to support their own currencies, to provide money for the purchase of oil (which is traded in dollars), and for other problems that have emerged as the crisis has spread to every corner of the globe. If the Bank of England gets dollars in a swap, it can then loan the dollars to its own commercial banks, which might be fearful of lending to one another because of the crisis.

While the Fed was busy injecting money and lending capacity into the financial system, the Treasury Department, often in cooperation with the Fed, was doing the same thing. In the fall of 2008, Paulson and Bernanke tried to get Congress to approve a $700 million bank bailout package that gave the Treasury unsupervised authority to use the money as they saw fit to help troubled banks and any other business entity. Congress balked and demanded some oversight, but still the Treasury was given great authority over the allocated funds. It has used this power to make multibillion-dollar loans to investment banks, commercial banks, AIG, Chrysler, General Motors, and many other companies. Typically, it has received preferred stock in these businesses, making the government part owner of many enterprises—but without voting rights. Money has been loaned so that one bank can take over another. Various plans have been made whereby the government will buy gobs of troubled assets from financial corporations, but so far these have foundered on the problem of valuing the toxic waste on corporate balance sheets.

Government regulatory agencies have already closed many problem banks, nationalizing them temporarily until their assets can be transferred to healthier institutions. In addition, Fannie Mae and Freddie Mac have been taken over directly by the government. However, the Treasury (and the president) has refused so far to nationalize the biggest troubled banks. In the Financial Stability Plan, announced on February 10, 2009, Secretary Geithner proposed a joint government-private fund to buy troubled assets from the many businesses that own them and would probably be declared insolvent if these assets were valued at what they would sell for today. To get hedge funds and other potential buyers to spend money for these assets, the government stands ready to loan them a high percentage of the money and assume a good deal of the risk. In a remarkable arrangement, the private buyers of the assets will make tons of money if the now toxic instruments someday rise in value, but the government (the public) will absorb most of the losses if they go down in value. As part of this plan, the Fed also will increase funding for TALF from $200 billion to one trillion dollars.

All told, the money either spent, committed, or available so far to getting the economy back on track is almost $15 trillion, an amount larger than the Gross Domestic Product.[39]

There are two things to note about all of these attempts to unfreeze credit markets. First, what the Fed and the Treasury have been doing is pumping several trillion dollars of new money into financial enterprises, and they have empowered themselves to put trillions more into the economy. Most people do not know that the Fed and the Treasury can pay for their programs by injecting into the economy the money in the vaults of the Federal Reserve banks or by printing new money (nothing backs this money other than our willingness to accept it as payment for our labor, for goods and services, for debts, for anything bought and sold). This is exactly what they have done. However, and second, none of these programs nor all of the money spent have helped get the economy back on track. The recipients of the cash have, for the most part, initially just hoarded it, afraid to lend it out. And consumers and businesses can't borrow much anyway, so strapped are they with debt and fear of the future. The truth is that in a period of rapidly rising pessimism and fear about the future, the demand for cash becomes insatiable; no matter how much more of it there is, those who have it will not readily spend it. So, the newly injected money can't significantly increase spending, output, and employment. But the real problem for the large banks has not been lack of liquidity—they are essentially insolvent, or bankrupt. Their assets are worth less than the amount of money they owe. Thus much of the money they have received appears to have gone down a black hole. In the future when banks report a profit, keep in mind that it will only be possible because the government has covered their losses in order to make them solvent, they don't count their bad debts, and the government has lent them money at close to zero interest.

The notion that the monetary authorities alone can end such a severe crisis has been pretty much discredited. The great economist John Maynard Keynes, writing during the Great Depression, said that in such circumstances, only massive fiscal stimulus, primarily in the form of new government spending, has any chance of working. In the recent past, most mainstream economists and all conservative politicians argued that if fiscal policy was needed to push up demand in the economy, it should be in the form of tax cuts. Tax reductions have become dogma for the right wing. There is scant evidence that the tax cuts engineered by Presidents Reagan and Bush Senior and Junior made the economy grow (although they certainly helped grow the Federal debt), but insistent propaganda by the right helped to provide cover for what these tax cuts really accomplished, namely a massive transfer of income from the bottom to the top. This redistribution of income and wealth is partly responsible for the troubles we are in now. Yet, the first thing President Bush agreed to when he realized that the economy was tanking was a tax rebate. This was approved by Congress in February of 2008. The money that taxpayers got did generate some spending, but not nearly enough. Too many households saved the money or reduced debt, neither of which created new demand and production.

As matters continued to deteriorate, more and more economists concluded that a very large dose of government spending, in addition to the hundreds of billions being thrown at the financial companies, was needed. There was a gigantic hole in the economy—several trillion dollars of consumer, investment, and export spending had disappeared and showed no sign of reappearing. Consumers were too much in debt; the value of their homes was falling; and they had lost or were in danger of losing their jobs. Businesses were suffering declining sales and lower profits. Why would they build new plants or purchase machinery? State and local governments were beginning to run large budget deficits, leading to the threat of large-scale layoffs and cuts in services. And the recession had spread from the United States to the rest of the world. This led to a fall in U.S. exports, which until mid-2008 were the only bright spot for U.S. companies. That left the government as the only viable source of demand for new output. Economists like Krugman and Stiglitz argued strongly for a very large dose of government spending, financed by borrowing, to jump-start the economy. Several kinds of spending were suggested, based on their likely impact on demand and employment:

- *Aid to state governments.* During a downturn, the taxes collected by state governments fall. Most states are legally mandated to balance their budgets, and this means that state spending will have to fall too. However, this only worsens the downturn, as public employees are laid off and spending projects are put on hold or cut back. Money from the federal government would alleviate these problems and boost overall spending and employment. (Even with the injection of funds from the national government that has occurred, many states are deep in debt. Some have reduced welfare and health spending for the poor and spending for education. Budget cuts in California will have drastic effects on many people—especially the most vulnerable.)

- *Direct aid to the unemployed.* Unemployment benefits run out when a recession lasts a long time. And as we have seen, many workers are not covered by the unemployment compensation system. Federal extensions of the time for which benefits are paid and incentives for the states (the system is administered by the states) to pay more generous benefits and make more people eligible would boost demand, because the unemployed will almost surely spend all of any added money they get. The same logic applies to all direct aid to the poor.

- *Mortgage relief.* Millions of home owners are heading for foreclosure, and millions more can barely pay their mortgages. Relief for them could take the form of lower interest rates, reductions in the principal owed on mortgages, and a change in bankruptcy law that would allow judges to adjust mortgage terms.

- *Infrastructure spending.* The roads, bridges, ports, sewage systems, schools, hospitals, communications and energy networks, and public transit systems are all in need of repair, upgrade, and expansion. Federal spending on these, especially those that are already in the planning pipeline, could have a dramatic impact on spending and employment. The Obama administration has made a commitment to the creation of so-called green jobs. These might include building energy-efficient cars; developing, making, and installing the machines and products that will transmit alternative energy, such as solar and wind power; retrofitting old buildings and houses, and similar types of projects.

All government spending has what is called a multiplier effect. A million dollars spent on bridge repair is a million-dollar increase in demand and output. Then, this is augmented by the spending of the workers who are paid to repair the bridges and prepare the materials. The money that workers spend then circulates through the economy—to a store, the store's employees, and so on.

President Obama promised a fiscal stimulus during the campaign in 2008, and he put together a team of economic advisors to construct one. His plan was too timid, and he made severe compromises with Republicans to try to get bipartisan support. The end result, $787 billion over a two-year period, was a hodgepodge of government transfers (to the states and the unemployed, for example), public spending, and tax cuts. It was made into law in February of 2009. Only three Republican senators voted for it (and no Republicans in the House of Representatives), and several Republican governors actually vowed to reject some of the federal aid, and one, Sanford of South Carolina (since disgraced by an extramarital affair), has been forced by his state supreme court to accept the money. The overall package is almost certainly too small to fill the spending gap (particularly as 40 percent was in the form of tax cuts, not spending), and full of useless tax cuts and incentives for businesses. To appease conservative critics, Obama has been quick to point out that 90 percent of the four million jobs the stimulus package is supposed to create will be in the private sector, where there will be no guarantees of decent wages, hours, and benefits. And he has already abandoned his strong support for the Employee Free Choice Act, which would make it easier for private sector workers to unionize. The president also announced on February 18, 2009, the Homeowner Affordability and Stability Plan, to give the types of relief to at-risk home owners described above. This initiative has brought a firestorm of criticism from the right, with the reactionaries saying that the plan will be a gift to those who took on mortgages beyond their means. But the plan was missing what was supposed to be its centerpiece—the ability of judges to lower the amount individuals owe on their homes. This provision of the bill was defeated by a massive lobbying effort by the financial industry, which may be weakened but still retains a huge amount of power in Washington. (It is, of course, absurd that during bankruptcy proceedings, judges have the power to reduce the amount an individual owes on a second home or a boat—but not on a primary residence.) At the time we're writing this book—June of 2009—a minuscule number of people have been helped by programs to keep them in their homes by renegotiating their mortgages. Other policies have also proven to be insufficient. For example, the money allocated to help states has proven woefully deficient. Even with the injection of funds from the national government many states are deep in debt. Some have reduced welfare and health spending for the poor and spending for education. The draconian budget cuts to education and social assistance programs in California will have drastic effects on many people—especially the most vulnerable.

It is impossible in a short book like this to enumerate all of the government's efforts to end this crisis. It seems that a new plan or program was proposed or put in place nearly every day. But just as monetary policy has failed so far to stem the tide, so too has fiscal policy proved ineffective. Things appear to have stabalized and may get better, but they are still deteriorating as far as the majority of population is concerned. As of August 2009, the numbers of unemployed are still increasing and it is not at all clear how many of nearly 7 million U.S. jobs lost in the recession so far will be recovered or when that might happen. When those working part-time but wanting full-time work and those that have stopped looking for work are added to the "officially" unemployed, the economy needs 30 million jobs right now to employ all those needing work! What will be the engine that propels growth and allows creation of new jobs to employ this mass of people? Will consumers just getting out from under massive debts and foreclosures really want to, or be able to, take on new debt in order to allow them to increase their consumption? Most likely they will not. In addition, there are no industries, including renewable energy companies, that appear able to supply the number of needed jobs. Thus, the future prospects for many people in our society do not appear bright.

13. Summary and Conclusions

There is no magic road out of the stagnation that has gripped the capitalist world. That being the case, what is needed is a redirection of priorities. Our real problems in America are not located in the stock market and other gambling casinos, but in what a large segment of the population faces every day: hunger, homelessness, inadequate health care, joblessness.

For now, we need a new New Deal—one that includes Government-created jobs and income support for the poor. What is ultimately needed: a new social system, in which production is for use instead of for profits.

—HARRY MAGDOFF, 1987

The capitalist economies of the world are in deep trouble. Some economists thought that the linkages between the United States and the rest of the world had been weakened as other nations gained more economic autonomy. A decoupling thesis was presented that claimed that a crisis in one part of the system—say North America—would not affect other major parts—say Europe and Asia. We now know this is not true. Toxic assets were sold around the world, and banks in Europe, Asia, and Japan are in trouble, too. Housing bubbles have burst in Ireland, Spain, and many other countries. In Eastern Europe, homes were bought with loans from Swiss, Austrian, and other European banks, payable in European currencies. As the economies of Hungary and other nations in the region, which financed their explosive growth with heavy borrowing from Western banks, have gone into recession, their currencies have suffered a sharp deterioration in exchange rates. This means that mortgage payments have risen sharply, as it now takes many more units of local currency to buy the Swiss francs or euros needed to pay the loans. In some cases, mortgage payments have doubled. Many countries embraced neoliberalism as fervently as the United States, and now they are paying the piper for years of deregulation. The most extreme case so far is Iceland, which actually went bankrupt and had to seek help from the International Monetary Fund. Countries that relied heavily on exports, such as Germany, Japan, and China, are facing seriously eroded economic conditions as U.S. consumers, once the world's buyers, sharply cut their spending. International economic linkages are working to make the crisis intractable. When something bad happens in one place, it reverberates in many other places. Declining demand in the United States causes lower incomes elsewhere, and these cause incomes here to fall further, and on and on. If Hungarians default on their mortgages, Swiss and German banks might fail, and this will cause trouble for U.S. banks, and on and on. But in the spring of 2009 the IMF, with newly infused funds from the European community, allowed Eastern Europe to step "back from the brink of collapse" (according to the *Wall Street Journal*) by providing loans to Hungary, Belarus, the Ukraine, Latvia, Serbia, Romania, and Poland.

Drastic actions are needed, even on capitalism's own terms. There is no doubt that the most efficient and straightforward way to proceed would have been for the federal government to nationalize some large banks, wipe out their shareholders, and put them on a firm footing. The U.S. auto industry must be both saved and transformed, lest millions more become unemployed. A national health care plan is mandatory, both to lower business costs and to keep workers healthy. Home owners must get some relief, and household debt must be reduced if demand is ever to be robust again. Ideally, the financial system should be strictly regulated if capitalism is to avoid future bubbles (though such strict regulation is probably impossible under the present system). The obscenely unequal distributions of income and wealth have to be dramatically changed if some sort of balanced growth is to take place. Wages have to rise for the same reason, as well as to reduce the debt burdens now choking so many working-class families.

The trouble is that even though these changes might help develop a more robust capitalism, from the perspective of the capitalists themselves most of these actions are not desirable—nor is it very likely that they can or will be made. Businesses find themselves inside a system based upon vicious competition, a "beggar thy neighbor" enterprise writ large. What is more, every sector of business has a hold on some politicians and influence in every public agency. Washington is teeming with lobbyists, and these people often write the legislation that is supposed to be in the public interest. No matter what the government initiative, self-interested parties try, and often succeed in, bending the legislation and its implementation to suit their needs. We can't have a true national health care system because the insurance and drug companies, plus their allies in medicine, won't stand for it and have the power to prevent it. The government cannot get the financial system in order because politicians are much too cozy with the bankers they regulate. Private housing inter-

THIS CRISIS HITS EVERYONE

An article appeared in the *The New Yorker* magazine about a slum in India on the property of Mumbai's airport. It describes how the people who live there are connected to the world economic downturn. Although they make their living by collecting recyclables from garbage, the downturn affects them, too. According to one of the inhabitants who reads the Tamil-language newspapers, "The banks in America went in a loss, then the big people went in a loss, then the scrap market in the slum areas came down, too." The article continues: "A kilo of empty water bottles, once worth twenty-five rupees, was now worth ten. This is how the crisis was understood."[40]

ests stand ready to stop public housing. The same is true for public transit and just about any other good thing you can name. If the new administration moves strongly to combat global warming and build a greener economy, we can be assured that no matter the gravity of the problem, the calculus of private interest will win out in the end. From society's point of view, and certainly from the perspective of workers, capitalism is an irrational system.

And if all of this is not problem enough, there remains the underlying tendency toward slow growth or stagnation. Even the stimulus package proposed by President Obama will not solve the fundamental stagnation problem, although it may help a large number of people. In addition, some help and comfort can be provided through extending unemployment benefits and increasing funds to programs such as food stamps and providing jobs through spending programs that will provide or keep a certain number of jobs. The original Great Depression programs didn't end the Depression, so is there any reason to suppose that government programs will end this one? It is true that the Great Depression work programs were nowhere near large enough to bring back prosperity. But today, even with the insights of John Maynard Keynes and decades of economic research, the fiscal package of spending programs, tax cuts, and deficit-financing are, according to the best and brightest mainstream economists, inadequate to the task at hand: replacing several trillion dollars' worth of reduced spending by the private economy as well as state and local governments. That the United States government is not going to do what would have to be done to end the Great Recession will not be surprising to readers who understand why the Great Depression did not end until the "epoch-making" spending of the Second World War did the job. Profit-seeking private interests always stood in the way. And unfortunately, the U.S. stimulus package is very much larger than that of the European Union or Japan.

The U.S. economy is in for a long period of anemic growth and high unemployment. There are no obvious sources of demand that will grow enough to overcome the many factors repressing demand. It is not clear what, if anything, can replace the huge growth of debt, speculation, and bubbles that propelled the economy for so many years. Hard times have come, and hard times are ahead. Certainly governments here and elsewhere have and will continue to do things that spur some growth and alleviate some of the misery. And it may be that another bubble will develop, perhaps based on some sort of "greening" of capitalism, spurred by large government spending. Then the process will begin again, with who knows what ending. In this regard, it is deeply troubling to observe that economic policy appears to be subservient to the same financial interests that brought us to such a sorry state in the first place. The federal government seems unwilling to step too hard on the toes of finance, and has larded nearly every one of its programs with significant monetary incentives for the big banks and other financial firms. We are either giving them money outright or making loans available at bargain basement interest rates, but we are not making demands on them to change their ways. The idea seems to be to return the financial system to its pre-crisis structure. If this isn't a recipe for a disastrous future reprise of what is happening now, we don't know what is.

But let us ask ourselves an important question. Is the roller-coaster ride that is capitalism what we want? Suppose that in a few years somehow things got back to "normal," with the GDP growing at between 2.5 and 3 percent, with unemployment between 4 and 5 percent, with wages growing only enough to keep up with inflation. Suppose even that we have a better health care system than we have now (although at present it seems that any improvements will be modest at best). What then? The "health" of the U.S. economy now depends on increasing exploitation at work supposedly compensated for through ever-rising private consumption. What have been the consequences of this? Longer, harder hours have compromised the health and quality of life of workers, reducing their best hours to meaningless drudgery at best. Rising consumption has polluted our planet; it has filled our houses with junk we never use; it has forced us to think we need bigger and bigger houses, which in turn has compelled us to move into the suburbs and exurbs, wasting power and water, creating vast expanses of ugly developments, and destroying much of our natural habitat. Consumption by individuals based on their purchasing power always relegates collective needs and collective consumption to second place, because it increases the political power of the businesses that benefit most from a system based on private profit. The system's need for ever-growing private consumption also encourages an exploding sales effort, to convince us to keep up the buying that will keep the profits flowing and the economic ball rolling. Advertising and the products it promotes must always be "new" and "advanced," to entice us to buy, although in reality this means that goods and services must become quickly obsolete or perceived to be so. The entire system becomes one of making things, throwing them away, and making new ones. Waste begetting waste, begetting still more waste.

It is impossible for ever-higher levels of consumption to make us happy. The logic of the system is that we must be perpetually unsatisfied, always wanting more. In a system that guarantees considerable inequality, we are bound to be envious of the consumption of those richer than we are. But every time we think we have caught up, we see that there are still many richer people above us. And if those below catch up with us, we have to consume more to stay ahead. It could be argued that a consumption-based society would be more acceptable if there were a rough equality of spending power. But this is—and cannot help but be—the case; capital accumulation will not allow it. We are not and cannot be "slouching toward utopia," to use the inapt phrase of economist J. Bradford DeLong, a utopia of a worldwide majority middle class of happy consumers, all buying big-screen televisions and nice automobiles. And does DeLong imagine that the world could ecologically support several billion human beings consuming at a pace on par with middle-class U.S. households? It is estimated that it would take the resources of four worlds like ours to provide the equivalent of a U.S. middle-class consumption pattern for all of the world's 6.5 billion people. Now, we are certainly not arguing that everyone should be poor or that those now at the bottom don't need a healthy dose of consumption, especially food, clothing, and shelter. But we are saying that the so-called consumer culture that characterizes the United States and a few other rich countries is not a model worth fighting for, nor is it ecologically sustainable.

What *is* worth fighting for? Perhaps this severe recession offers us an opportunity to ask this question. This crisis has revealed the rotten foundation of our economy and called into question the neoliberal policies and ideology that have deepened the rot. We cannot sustain ourselves with ever-larger doses of debt relative to the underlying economy. We cannot be happy in a world of rising insecurity: How will we pay the debts? Where will we find decent and secure employment? How will we cope with health problems? How will we survive old age? Will our air, water, and food supply be poisoned? We cannot be happy in a world in which the fruits of human labor are distributed in an obscenely unequal manner. Inequality itself causes a host of problems, from lower life expectancies of those further down the ladder to more people in prison, and it raises the level of insecurity. The rage of the poor and the fear of the rich are the legacies of the growing gap between them. Finally, and of the greatest importance, we cannot be happy with the nature of the work most of us are compelled to do. Millions of us are unemployed, and this is a bad thing. But for those working, the stress is rising, as fewer people are being forced to do more work and employment becomes more precarious. Employers use periods like this to discover ways to permanently reduce the size of their workforces. They continue the strategy of lean production, using as little skilled labor as possible, constantly stressing the system so that work can be sped up, and then cutting benefits as much as possible. There is no way that the majority of people can do meaningful work in a system like this. Labor is simply a cost of production, to be minimized and on a par with a piece of equipment or fuel. What does it mean when there is a joke that says, "The only thing worse than being employed is being unemployed"?

It seems to us that there are many things worth fighting for. Here is a list for starters. Readers will no doubt think of others.

- *Adequate food for everyone.* For fifty years, Cuba has provided a minimum food basket for each person. Imagine what a rich nation like the United States could do here. Food production and distribution should be studied with an eye toward producing all food as ecologically sound (perhaps organically) as possible and making sure that each and every person eats a varied and healthful diet.

- *Decent housing.* As we argued above, attractive and relatively inexpensive housing could be built by a public corporation, and workers could at the same time be trained to build and maintain them. Energy efficiency could be incorporated not only into the design of the houses but also into the layout of neighborhoods and public spaces. Existing buildings could be rehabilitated, and if some have to be demolished, all possible materials could be salvaged. Imagine how much housing could be built and rehabbed just with the money the government has given to the notorious AIG company.

- *Universal health care.* The health care system of the United States is a disgrace—wasteful, costly, and unequally distributed to an extreme degree. Human health cannot be subjected to the profit motive without dire consequences, as anyone who is sick and without money knows.

- *Full employment/good jobs.* Work is a necessary and essential human enterprise. It is the way we transform the world and the fundamental way in which we use our capacity to think and to do. Therefore employment that encourages the use of our full human capacities must be a right. The government must itself create as much socially useful employment as is necessary to achieve this goal. Good jobs must be those in which the hours of work are short enough to allow working people ample time for meaningful leisure. A shorter workweek and workday would have the added benefit of creating more jobs.

- *Quality education for all.* Education in the United States parallels health care in terms of its inadequacies. Good schooling cannot be based upon such inane principles as the cynically named No Child Left Behind Act. Education must build from the experiences of the students outward toward increasingly complex and abstract ideas.

Creativity, independence of mind, and healthy bodies must take center stage—in buildings and surroundings that are conducive to learning.

- *Adequate income in old age.* The current Social Security system is perhaps the best-managed enterprise in the federal government. It is a universal system that provides essential resources—retirement, disability income, health care, funds for minor survivors—to tens of millions of persons. It is a system that could and should be made much more generous.

- *Enhanced public transportation.* All manner of efficient, energy-conserving, cheap, and high-speed public transportation should be built, in as many places as possible.

- *A commitment to a sustainable environment.* Whatever increases the pollution of our water, land, and air must be rejected. Clean air, water, and soil and well-working ecosystems are essential for our survival as well as the survival of many other species. Whatever raises the earth's temperature must be rejected. We must stop thinking of our natural resources as private property, to be endlessly exploited and polluted, and begin thinking of them as the wealth of us all.

- *Progressive taxation.* We have seen in this Great Recession that we have been robbed and cheated by a tiny minority of very rich people. These thieves have contributed nothing to social well-being, and in fact have greatly detracted from it. The incomes of the very rich should be punitively taxed, and a high degree of progressivity must be restored to the tax system. Whichever activities are aimed at merely short-term and socially unproductive gain must be heavily taxed.

- *A non-imperialist government.* There is every reason to believe that the foreign military operations of the United States are extraordinarily harmful to the people of both the rest of the world and to those in the United States. We must demand peace and an end to state violence. Period.

- *Labor- and environment-friendly trade.* Trade among nations and movements of people from one country to another can be wonderful things. However, for this to be so, economic relationships among nations must be based on the fact that human beings and Mother Earth are the basis of all production and exchange. Concern for both must be central to all economic relationships, within and among nations.

Can these goals be achieved inside the present economic system? Perhaps some can in very limited ways, but most of them clearly cannot. The system simply will not allow it. Pragmatists say that these things are utopian, that we have to work within the system and achieve what we can gradually and in a piecemeal fashion. It seems to us, however, that this view is utopian. We have to stick to our principles, come hell or high water. Only if we do can we keep this economic system on trial, challenging it to actually satisfy the basic needs of all the people. We may even get a few crumbs from those who control the political economy, if only to subdue and pacify us. But if we steadfastly continue to demand what should be ours by right, by virtue of the fact that we are human beings, we will push the system into a crisis of legitimacy. Then, as people begin to see that this system can never deliver what is needed for us to realize our capacities and enjoy our lives, they will begin to consider and put into practice alternative mechanisms of production and distribution, those that are democratically controlled and have as their aim the achievement of maximum human happiness: an economy and society in which, instead of private gain, the purpose is to serve the needs of the people, because it is truly of the people, by providing the necessities of life for all, without promoting excessive consumption (consumerism) while protecting earth's life support systems. In other words, socialism.

APPENDIX

A Timeline of the Financial Crisis and the Great Recession

APRIL 2007

New Century Financial Corporation, a leading subprime mortgage lender, files for Chapter 11 bankruptcy protection.

JULY 2007

Bear Stearns liquidates two hedge funds that invested in various types of mortgage-backed securities.

AUGUST 2007

American Home Mortgage Investment Corporation files for Chapter 11 bankruptcy protection.

SEPTEMBER 2007

The Chancellor of the Exchequer authorizes the Bank of England to provide liquidity support for Northern Rock, the United Kingdom's fifth-largest mortgage lender.

The Federal Reserve Board votes to reduce the primary credit rate to 5.25 percent.

OCTOBER 2007

The Federal Reserve Board votes to reduce the primary credit rate to 5.00 percent.

DECEMBER 2007

Recession begins—decided a year after the fact by the Business Cycle Dating Committee of the National Bureau of Economic Research.

The Federal Reserve Board votes to reduce the primary credit rate to 4.75 percent.

The Federal Reserve Board announces the creation of a Term Auction Facility (TAF) in which fixed amounts of term funds will be auctioned to depository institutions against a wide variety of collateral. The Federal Reserve Board announces that TAF auctions will be conducted every two weeks as long as financial market conditions warrant.

JANUARY 2008

Bank of America announces that it will purchase Countrywide Financial in an all-stock transaction worth approximately $4 billion.

FEBRUARY 2008

President Bush signs the Economic Stimulus Act of 2008 (Public Law 110-185) into law.

Northern Rock is taken into state ownership by the Treasury of the United Kingdom.

MARCH 2008

Carlyle Capital Corporation receives a default notice after failing to meet margin calls on its mortgage bond fund.

The Federal Reserve Board announces $50 billion TAF auctions and extends the TAF for at least six months. The Board also initiates a series of term repurchase transactions, expected to cumulate to $100 billion, conducted as 28-day term repurchase agreements with primary dealers.

The Federal Reserve Board announces the creation of the Term Securities Lending Facility (TSLF), which will lend up to $200 billion of Treasury securities for 28-day terms against federal agency debt, federal agency residential mortgage-backed securities (MBS), non-agency AAA/Aaa private label residential MBS, and other securities.

The Federal Reserve Board approves the financing arrangement announced by JPMorgan Chase and Bear Stearns. The Federal Reserve Board also announces they are "monitoring market developments closely and will continue to provide liquidity as necessary to promote the orderly function of the financial system."

The Federal Reserve Board establishes the Primary Dealer Credit Facility (PDCF), extending credit to primary dealers at the primary credit rate against a broad range of investment grade securities.

The Federal Reserve Board twice votes to reduce the primary credit rate, ending at 2.50 percent.

The Federal Reserve Bank of New York announces that it will provide term financing to facilitate JPMorgan Chase's acquisition of Bear Stearns Companies Inc. A limited liability company (Maiden Lane) is formed to control $30 billion of Bear Stearns assets that are pledged as security for $29 billion in term financing from the New York Fed at its primary credit rate. JPMorgan Chase will assume the first $1 billion of any losses on the portfolio.

APRIL 2008

The Federal Reserve Board votes to reduce the primary credit rate to 2.25 percent.

JUNE 2008

The Federal Reserve Board announces approval of the notice of Bank of America to acquire Countrywide Financial Corporation.

JULY 2008

President Bush signs into law the Housing and Economic Recovery Act of 2008 (Public Law 110-289), which, among other provisions, authorizes the Treasury to purchase GSE obligations and reforms the regulatory supervision of the GSEs under a new Federal Housing Finance Agency.

SEPTEMBER 2008

The Federal Housing Finance Agency (FHFA) places Fannie Mae and Freddie Mac in government conservatorship.

Bank of America announces its intent to purchase Merrill Lynch for $50 billion.

Lehman Brothers Holdings Inc. files for Chapter 11 bankruptcy protection.

The Federal Reserve Board authorizes the Federal Reserve Bank of New York to lend up to $85 billion to the American International Group (AIG).

The U.S. Treasury Department announces a Supplementary Financing Program consisting of a series of Treasury bill issues that will provide cash for use in Federal Reserve initiatives.

The Federal Reserve Board approves applications of investment banking companies Goldman Sachs and Morgan Stanley to become bank holding companies.

The U.S. Treasury Department opens its Temporary Guarantee Program for Money Market Funds. The temporary guarantee program provides coverage to shareholders for amounts they hold in participating money market funds.

The FDIC announces that Citigroup will purchase the banking operations of Wachovia Corporation.

The U.S. House of Representatives rejects legislation submitted by the Treasury Department requesting authority to purchase troubled assets from financial institutions.

OCTOBER 2008

Congress passes and President Bush signs into law the Emergency Economic Stabilization Act of 2008 (Public Law 110-343), which establishes the $700 billion Troubled Asset Relief Program (TARP).

The Federal Reserve Board announces the creation of the Commercial Paper Funding Facility (CPFF), which will provide a liquidity backstop to U.S. issuers of commercial paper through a special purpose vehicle that will purchase three-month unsecured and asset-backed commercial paper directly from eligible issuers.

The FDIC announces an increase in deposit insurance coverage to $250,000 per depositor as authorized by the Emergency Economic Stabilization Act of 2008.

The Federal Reserve Board authorizes the Federal Reserve Bank of New York to borrow up to $37.8 billion in investment-grade, fixed-income securities from American International Group (AIG) in return for cash collateral.

The Federal Reserve Board reduces the primary credit rate first to 1.75 percent and then to 1.25 percent.

PNC Financial Services Group Inc. purchases National City Corporation, creating the fifth largest U.S. bank.

The International Monetary Fund (IMF) announces the creation of a short-term liquidity facility for market-access countries.

NOVEMBER 2008

The Federal Reserve Board and the U.S. Treasury Department announce a restructuring of the government's financial support of AIG. The Treasury will purchase $40 billion of AIG preferred shares under the TARP program, a portion of which will be used to reduce the Federal Reserve's loan to AIG from $85 billion to $60 billion. The terms of the loan are modified to reduce the interest rate and lengthen the term of the loan from two to five years. The Federal Reserve Board also authorizes the Federal Reserve Bank of New York to establish two new lending facilities for AIG: the Residential Mortgage-Backed Securities Facility will lend up to $22.5 billion to a newly formed limited liability company (LLC) to purchase residential MBS from AIG; the Collateralized Debt Obligations Facility will lend up to $30 billion to a newly formed LLC to purchase CDOs from AIG (Maiden Lane III LLC).

U.S. Treasury secretary Paulson formally announces that the Treasury has decided not to use TARP funds to purchase illiquid mortgage-related assets from financial institutions.

The U.S. Treasury Department purchases a total of $33.5 billion in preferred stock in 21 U.S. banks under the Capital Purchase Program.

Three large U.S. life insurance companies seek TARP funding: Lincoln National, Hartford Financial Services Group, and Genworth Financial. They announce their intentions to purchase lenders/depositories and thus qualify as savings and loan companies to access TARP funding.

Executives of Ford, General Motors, and Chrysler testify before Congress, requesting access to the TARP for federal loans.

Fannie Mae and Freddie Mac announce that they will suspend mortgage foreclosures until January 2009.

The U.S. Treasury Department announces that it will help liquidate the Reserve Fund's U.S. Government Fund. The Treasury agrees to serve as a buyer of last resort for the fund's securities to ensure the orderly liquidation of the fund.

The U.S. Treasury Department purchases a total of $3 billion in preferred stock in 23 U.S. banks under the Capital Purchase Program.

The U.S. Treasury Department, Federal Reserve Board, and FDIC jointly announce an agreement with Citigroup to provide a package of guarantees, liquidity access, and capital. Citigroup will issue preferred shares to the Treasury and FDIC in exchange for protection against losses on a $306 billion pool of commercial and residential securities held by Citigroup. The Federal Reserve will backstop residual risk in the asset pool through a non-recourse loan. In addition, the Treasury will invest an additional $20 billion in Citigroup from the TARP.

The Federal Reserve Board announces the creation of the Term Asset-Backed Securities Lending Facility (TALF), under which the Federal Reserve Bank of

New York will lend up to $200 billion on a non-recourse basis to holders of AAA-rated asset-backed securities and recently originated consumer and small business loans. The U.S. Treasury will provide $20 billion of TARP money for credit protection.

The Federal Reserve Board announces a new program to purchase direct obligations of housing related government-sponsored enterprises (GSEs)—Fannie Mae, Freddie Mac, and Federal Home Loan Banks—and MBS backed by the GSEs. Purchases of up to $100 billion in GSE direct obligations will be conducted as auctions among Federal Reserve primary dealers. Purchases of up to $500 billion in MBS will be conducted by asset managers.

The Federal Reserve Board announces approval of the notice of Bank of America Corporation to acquire Merrill Lynch and Company.

DECEMBER 2008

The U.S. Treasury Department purchases a total of $4 billion in preferred stock in 35 U.S. banks under the Capital Purchase Program.

The U.S. Treasury Department purchases a total of $6.25 billion in preferred stock in 28 U.S. banks under the Capital Purchase Program.

The Federal Reserve Board announces that it has approved the application of PNC Financial Services to acquire National City Corporation.

The Federal Reserve Board reduces the primary credit rate to 0.50 percent.

The U.S. Treasury Department authorizes loans of up to $13.4 billion for General Motors and $4 billion for Chrysler from the TARP.

The U.S. Treasury Department purchases a total of $27.9 billion in preferred stock in 49 U.S. banks under the Capital Purchase Program.

The Federal Reserve Board approves the application of CIT Group Inc., an $81 billion financing company, to become a bank holding company. The Board cites "unusual and exigent circumstances affecting the financial markets" for expeditious action on CIT Group's application.

The U.S. Treasury Department purchases a total of $15.1 billion in preferred stock from 43 U.S. banks under the Capital Purchase Program.

The Federal Reserve Board approves the applications of GMAC LLC and IB Finance Holding Company, LLC (IBFHC) to become bank holding companies on conversion of GMAC Bank, a $33 billion Utah industrial loan company, to a commercial bank. GMAC Bank is a direct subsidiary of IBFHC and an indirect subsidiary of GMAC LLC, a $211 billion company. The Board cites "unusual and exigent circumstances affecting the financial markets" for expeditious action on these applications. As part of the agreement, General Motors will reduce its ownership interest in GMAC to less than 10 percent.

The U.S. Treasury Department announces that it will purchase $5 billion in equity from GMAC as part of its program to assist the domestic automotive industry. The Treasury also agrees to lend up to $1 billion to General Motors.

The U.S. Securities and Exchange Commission (SEC) releases a report that recommends against the suspension of fair value accounting standards. The report was mandated by the Emergency Economic Stabilization Act of 2008 (EESA).

The U.S. Treasury Department purchases a total of $1.91 billion in preferred stock from seven U.S. banks under the Capital Purchase Program.

JANUARY 2009

The Federal Reserve Bank of New York begins purchasing fixed-rate mortgage-backed securities guaranteed by Fannie Mae, Freddie Mac and Ginnie Mae under a program first announced on November 25, 2008.

The U.S. Treasury Department purchases a total of $4.8 billion in preferred stock from 43 U.S. banks under the Capital Purchase Program.

At the request of President-elect Obama, President Bush submits a request to Congress for the remaining $350 billion in TARP funding for use by the incoming administration.

The U.S. Treasury Department purchases a total of $1.4 billion in preferred stock from 39 U.S. banks under the Capital Purchase Program.

The Treasury, Federal Reserve, and FDIC announce a package of guarantees, liquidity access, and capital for Bank of America. The Treasury and the FDIC will enter a loss-sharing arrangement with Bank of America on a $118 billion portfolio of loans, securities, and other assets in exchange for preferred shares. In addition, and if necessary, the Federal Reserve will provide a non-recourse loan to backstop residual risk in the portfolio. Separately, the Treasury will invest $20 billion in Bank of America from the TARP in exchange for preferred stock.

The Treasury Department announces that it will lend $1.5 billion from the TARP to a special purpose entity created by Chrysler Financial to finance the extension of new consumer auto loans.

The U.S. Treasury Department purchases a total of $326 million in preferred stock from 23 U.S. banks under the Capital Purchase Program.

U.S. Treasury Department purchases a total of $1.15 billion in preferred stock from 42 U.S. banks under the Capital Purchase Program.

FEBRUARY 2009

The Federal Reserve Board releases additional terms and conditions of the Term Asset-Backed Securities Loan Facility (TALF). Under the TALF, the Federal Reserve Bank of New York will lend up to $200 billion to eligible owners of certain AAA-rated asset-backed securities backed by newly and recently originated auto loans, credit card loans, student loans, and SBA-guaranteed small business loans.

The U.S. Treasury Department purchases a total of $238.5 million in preferred stock from 28 U.S. banks under the Capital Purchase Program.

Treasury secretary Timothy Geithner announces a Financial Stability Plan involving Treasury purchases of convertible preferred stock in eligible banks, the creation of a Public-Private Investment Fund to acquire troubled loans and other assets from financial institutions, expansion of the Federal Reserve's Term Asset-Backed Securities Loan Facility (TALF), and new initiatives to stem residential mortgage foreclosures and to support small business lending.

The Federal Reserve Board announces that it is prepared to expand the Term Asset-Backed Securities Loan Facility (TALF) to as much as $1 trillion and broaden the eligible collateral to include AAA-rated commercial mortgage-backed securities, private-label residential mortgage-backed securities, and other asset-backed securities. An expansion of the TALF would be supported by $100 billion from the Troubled Asset Relief Program (TARP). The Federal Reserve Board will announce the date that the TALF will commence operations later this month.

The U.S. Treasury Department purchases a total of $429 million in preferred stock from 29 U.S. banks under the Capital Purchase Program.

MARCH 2009

The Treasury Department and Federal Reserve Board announce a restructuring of the government's assistance to American International Group (AIG). Under the restructuring, AIG will receive as much as $30 billion of additional capital from the Troubled Asset Relief Program (TARP). In addition, the Treasury Department will exchange its existing $40 billion cumulative preferred shares in AIG for new preferred shares with revised terms that more closely resemble common equity. Finally, AIG's revolving credit facility with the Federal Reserve Bank of New York will be reduced from $60 billion to no less than $25 billion and the terms will be modified. In exchange, the Federal Reserve will receive preferred interests in two special-purpose vehicles created to hold the outstanding common stock of two subsidiaries of AIG: American Life Insurance Company and American International Assurance Company Ltd. Separately, AIG reports a fourth-quarter 2008 loss of $61.7 billion, and a loss of $99.3 billion for all of 2008.

The Treasury Department and the Federal Reserve Board announce the launch of the Term Asset-Backed Securities Loan Facility (TALF). Under the program, the Federal Reserve Bank of New York will lend up to $200 billion to eligible owners of certain AAA-rated asset-backed securities backed by newly and recently originated auto loans, credit card loans, student loans and small business loans that are guaranteed by the Small Business Administration. The Federal Reserve and Treasury expect to include asset-backed securities backed by other types of loans in future monthly fundings. Subscriptions for funding in March will be accepted on March 17, 2009. Securitizations will be funded by the program on March 25, 2009. The program will hold monthly fundings through December 2009 or longer if extended by the Federal Reserve Board.

The Treasury Department announces guidelines to enable servicers to begin modifications of eligible mortgages under the Homeowner Affordability and Stability Plan.

The U.S. Treasury Department purchases a total of $284.7 million in preferred stock from 22 U.S. banks under the Capital Purchase Program.

Freddie Mac announces that it had a net loss of $23.9 billion in the fourth quarter of 2008, and a net loss of $50.1 billion for 2008 as a whole. Further, Freddie Mac announces that its conservator has submitted a request to the U.S. Treasury Department for an additional $30.8 billion in funding for the company under the Senior Preferred Stock Purchase Agreement with the Treasury.

The U.S. Treasury Department purchases a total of $1.45 billion in preferred stock from 19 U.S. banks under the Capital Purchase Program.

The Federal Deposit Insurance Corporation (FDIC) decides to extend the debt guarantee portion of the Temporary Liquidity Guarantee Program (TLGP) from June 30, 2009, through October 31, 2009, and to impose a surcharge on debt issued with a maturity of one year or more beginning in the second quarter of 2009 to gradually phase out the program.

The Federal Open Market Committee (FOMC) decides to increase the size of the Federal Reserve's balance sheet by purchasing up to an additional $750 billion of agency mortgage-backed securities, bringing its total purchases of these securities up to $1.25 trillion this year, and to increase its purchases of agency debt this year by up to $100 billion to a total of up to $200 billion. The FOMC also decides to purchase up to $300 billion of longer-term Treasury securities over the next six months to help improve conditions in private credit markets. Finally, the FOMC announces that it anticipates expanding the range of eligible collateral for the TALF (Term Asset-Backed Securities Loan Facility).

The U.S. Department of the Treasury announces an Auto Supplier Support Program that will provide up to $5 billion in financing to the automotive industry. The Supplier Support Program will provide selected suppliers with financial protection on monies (receivables) they are owed by domestic auto companies and the opportunity to access immediate liquidity against those obligations. Receivables created with respect to goods shipped after March 19, 2009, will be eligible for the program. Any domestic auto company is eligible to participate in the program. Any U.S.-based supplier that ships to a participating auto manufacturer on qualifying commercial terms may be eligible to participate in the program.

The Federal Reserve Board announces an expansion of the eligible collateral for loans extended by the Term Asset-Backed Securities Loan Facility (TALF) to include asset-backed securities backed by mortgage servicing advances, loans or leases related to business equipment, leases of vehicle fleets, and floor-plan loans (for financing of wholesale vehicle inventories). The new categories of collateral will be eligible for the April TALF funding.

The Federal Reserve Bank of New York releases the initial results of the first round of loan requests for funding from the Term Asset-Backed Securities Loan Facility (TALF). The amount of TALF loans requested at the March 17–19 operation was $4.7 billion.

The FDIC completes the sale of IndyMac Federal Bank to OneWest Bank. OneWest will assume all deposits of IndyMac, and the 33 branches of IndyMac will reopen as branches of OneWest on March 20. As of January 31, 2009, IndyMac had total assets of $23.5 billion and total deposits of $6.4 billion. IndyMac reported fourth-quarter 2008 losses of $2.6 billion, and the total estimated loss to the Deposit Insurance Fund of the FDIC is $10.7 billion.

The U.S. Treasury Department purchases a total of $80.8 million in preferred stock from ten U.S. banks under the Capital Purchase Program.

The Treasury Department announces details on the Public-Private Investment Program for Legacy Assets. The program will have two parts: a Legacy Loans Program and a Legacy Securities Program. The Legacy Loans Program will facilitate the creation of individual Public-Private Investment Funds that will purchase distressed loans that are currently held by banks. The Treasury intends to provide 50 percent of the equity capital for each fund. The FDIC will provide oversight for the formation, funding, and operation of these funds, and guarantee the debt issued by the funds. Under the Legacy Securities Program, the Treasury Department will approve up to five asset managers who will have the opportunity to raise private capital to acquire distressed securities currently held by banks. The Treasury will provide 50 percent of the equity capital for each investment fund and will consider requests for loans to each fund. In addition, the investment funds would also be eligible for loans from the Term Asset-Backed Securities Facility (TALF).

The Treasury Department outlines a framework for comprehensive regulatory reform that focuses on containing systemic risks in the financial system. The framework calls for assigning responsibility over all systemically important firms and critical payment and settlement systems to a single independent regulator. Further, it calls for higher standards on capital and risk management for systemically important firms; for requiring all hedge funds above a certain size to register with a financial regulator; for a comprehensive framework of oversight, protection, and disclosure for the over-the-counter derivatives market; for new requirements for money market funds; and for stronger resolution authority covering all financial institutions that pose systemic risks to the economy.

The U.S. Treasury Department purchases a total of $193 million in preferred stock from 14 U.S. banks under the Capital Purchase Program.

The General Accounting Office (GAO) releases a report on the status of efforts to address transparency and accountability issues for the Troubled Asset Relief Program (TARP). The report provides information about the nature and purpose of TARP funding through March 27, 2009, the performance of the Treasury Department's Office of Financial Stability, and TARP performance indicators.

The U.S. Treasury Department announces an extension of its temporary Money Market Funds Guarantee Program through September 18, 2009. This program will continue to provide coverage to shareholders up to the amount held in participating money market funds as of the close of business on September 19, 2008. The Program currently covers over $3 trillion of combined fund assets and was scheduled to end on April 30, 2009.

Four bank holding companies announced that they had redeemed all of the preferred shares they issued to the U.S. Treasury under the Capital Purchase Program of the Troubled Asset Relief Program (TARP). The four banks are Bank of Marin Bancorp (Novato, CA); Iberiabank Corporation (Lafayette, LA); Old National Bancorp (Evansville, IN); and Signature Bank (New York, NY).

APRIL 2009

The Financial Accounting Standards Board approves new guidance to ease the accounting of troubled assets held by banks and other financial companies. In particular, the Board provides new guidance on how to determine the fair value of assets for which there is no active market.

The U.S. Treasury purchases a total of $54.8 million in preferred stock from 10 U.S. banks under the Capital Purchase Program.

The U.S. Treasury purchases a total of $22.8 million in preferred stock from 5 U.S. banks under the Capital Purchase Program.

The U.S. Treasury purchases a total of $40.9 million in preferred stock from 6 U.S. banks under the Capital Purchase Program.

The Federal Reserve Board publishes a white paper describing the process and methodologies employed by federal banking supervisory authorities in their forward-looking assessment (stress test) of large U.S. bank holding companies.

The U.S. Treasury purchases a total of $121.8 million in preferred stock from 12 U.S. banks under the Capital Purchase Program.

MAY 2009

The Federal Reserve Board announces that, starting in June, commercial mortgage-backed securities (CMBS) and securities backed by insurance premium finance loans will be eligible collateral under the Term Asset-Backed Securities Loan Facility (TALF). The Board also authorizes TALF loans with maturities of five years. Currently, all TALF loans have maturities of three years. TALF loans with five-year maturities will be available for the June funding to finance purchases of CMBS, ABS backed by student loans, and ABS backed by loans guaranteed by the Small Business Administration.

The U.S. Treasury purchases a total of $45.5 million in preferred stock from 7 U.S. banks under the Capital Purchase Program.

The Federal Reserve releases the results of the Supervisory Capital Assessment Program (stress test) of the 19 largest U.S. bank holding companies. The assessment finds that the 19 firms could lose $600 billion during 2009 and 2010 if the economy were to track the more adverse scenario considered in the program. The assessment also finds that 9 of the 19 firms already have adequate capital to maintain Tier 1 capital in excess of 6 percent of total assets and common equity capital in excess of 4 percent under the more adverse scenario. Ten firms would need to add $185 billion to their capital to maintain adequate buffers under the more adverse scenario. However, transactions and revenues since the end of 2008 have reduced to $75 billion the additional capital these firms must raise in order to establish the capital buffer required under the program. A bank holding company needing to augment its capital buffers will be required to develop a detailed plan to be approved by its primary supervisor within thirty days and to implement its plan to raise additional capital by early November 2009.

Fannie Mae reports a loss of $23.2 billion for the first quarter of 2009. The director of the Federal Housing Finance Agency (FHFA), which has been conservator of Fannie Mae since September 6, 2008, requests $19 billion from the U.S. Treasury Department under the terms of the Senior Preferred Stock Purchase

Agreement between Fannie Mae and the Treasury to eliminate the firm's net worth deficit. Separately, on May 6, 2009, the Treasury Department and the FHFA enter into an amendment to increase the Treasury's funding commitment to Fannie Mae to $200 billion from $100 billion, increase the allowed size of Fannie Mae's mortgage portfolio to $900 billion, and to increase the firm's allowable outstanding debt to $1,080 billion.

The U.S. Treasury purchases a total of $42 million in preferred stock from 7 U.S. banks under the Capital Purchase Program.

Freddie Mac reports a first-quarter 2009 loss of $9.9 billion and a net worth deficit of $6.0 billion as of March 31, 2009. The director of the Federal Housing Finance Agency (FHFA) submits a request to the U.S. Treasury Department for funding in the amount of $6.1 billion in his capacity as conservator of Freddie Mac. Further, the Treasury Department and FHFA, acting on Freddie Mac's behalf as its conservator, entered into an amendment to the Purchase Agreement between the company and Treasury that increases the Treasury's funding commitment to the firm to $200 billion from $100 billion, increases the allowed size of Freddie Mac's mortgage-related investments portfolio by $50 billion to $900 billion, and increases the firm's allowable debt outstanding to $1,080 billion until December 31, 2010.

The U.S. Treasury purchases a total of $107.6 million in preferred stock from 14 U.S. banks under the Capital Purchase Program.

The Federal Reserve Board announces that, starting in July, certain high-quality commercial mortgage-backed securities issued before January 1, 2009 (legacy CMBS) will become eligible collateral under the Term Asset-Backed Securities Loan Facility (TALF). The objective of the expansion is to restart the market for legacy securities and, by doing so, stimulate the extension of new credit by helping to ease balance sheet pressures on banks and other financial institutions. Eligible CMBS must have a triple-A rating from at least two major rating services.

President Obama signs the Helping Families Save Their Homes Act of 2009, which temporarily raises FDIC deposit insurance coverage from $100,000 per depositor to $250,000 per depositor. The new coverage at FDIC-insured institutions will expire on January 1, 2014, when the amount will return to its standard level of $100,000 per depositor for all account categories except IRAs and other certain retirement accounts.

The Federal Deposit Insurance Corporation (FDIC) announces the approval of GMAC Financial Services to participate in the Temporary Liquidity Guarantee Program (TLGP). GMAC will be allowed to issue up to $7.4 billion in new FDIC-guaranteed debt.

Standard and Poor's Ratings Services lowers its outlook on the United Kingdom government debt from stable to negative because of the estimated fiscal cost of supporting the nation's banking system. S & P estimates that this cost could double the government's debt burden to about 100 percent of GDP by 2013.

The Federal Reserve Board announces the adoption of a final rule that will allow bank holding companies to include in their Tier 1 capital without restriction senior perpetual preferred stock issued to the U.S. Treasury Department under the Troubled Asset Relief Program (TARP).

The FDIC announces that the number of "problem banks" increased from 252 insured institutions with $159 billion in assets at the end of the fourth quarter of 2008 to 305 institutions with $220 billion of assets at the end of the first quarter of 2009. The FDIC also announces that there were 21 bank failures in the first quarter of 2009, which is the largest number of failed institutions in the same time period since the first quarter of 1992 (during the savings and loan crisis).

JUNE 2009

As part of a new restructuring agreement with the U.S. Treasury and the governments of Canada and Ontario, General Motors Corporation and three domestic subsidiaries announce that they have filed for relief under Chapter 11 of the U.S. Bankruptcy Code.

The Federal Reserve Board announces the criteria it will use to evaluate redemption applications from the 19 bank holding companies that received U.S. Treasury capital as part of the Supervisory Capital Assessment Program.

The FDIC announces that the previously planned sale of impaired bank assets under the Legacy Loans Program (LLP) will be postponed. According to Chairman Bair: "Banks have been able to raise capital without having to sell bad assets through the LLP, which reflects renewed investor confidence in our banking system."

The Treasury Department announces that ten of the largest U.S. financial institutions participating in the Capital Purchase Program have met the requirements for repayment established by the primary federal banking supervisors. If these firms choose to repay the capital acquired through the program, the Treasury will receive up to $68 billion in repayment proceeds.

A Brief Bibliographical Study Guide

All study of capitalism, including its tendency toward crisis, must begin with Karl Marx's magisterial three-volume work, *Capital*, available in many editions and in most good libraries. Indeed, volume 1 might change your life. The theoretical perspective laid out in this book was best elucidated in Paul A. Baran and Paul M. Sweezy's *Monopoly Capital* (New York: Monthly Review Press, 1968). This seminal work is brought up to date to explain the current crisis in John Bellamy Foster and Fred Magdoff's *The Great Financial Crisis: Causes and Consequences* (New York: Monthly Review Press, 2009). A good introduction to both mainstream and radical economics that includes a discussion of neoliberalism is Michael D. Yates, *Naming the System* (New York: Monthly Review Press, 2002). Good articles on both capitalism and alternatives to it can be found in Fred Magdoff and Harry Magdoff, "Disposable Workers: Today's Reserve Army of Labor," *Monthly Review*, April 2004; and Harry Magdoff and Fred Magdoff, "Approaching Socialism," *Monthly Review*, July/August 2005. For the shocking story of how the financial sector has, in effect, taken over the U.S. government, read Simon Johnson, "The Quiet Coup," *The Atlantic Monthly*. May 2009. For an account of financial shenanigans large and small, see Michael Lewis's article, "The End," at http://www.portfolio.com/news-markets/national-news/portfolio/2008/11/11/The-End-of-Wall-Streets-Boom. A good article on the automobile industry is Herman Rosenfeld, "The North American Auto Industry in Crisis," *Monthly Review*, June 2009. Readers who want to keep abreast of economic matters should read newspapers such as the *New York Times*, *Wall Street Journal*, *Los Angeles Times*, and the *Guardian* (United Kingdom). The best mainstream U.S. economists on the current situation are Paul Krugman, Joseph Stiglitz, Herman Daly, and Nuriel Roubini. The magazine *Business Week* also contains much useful information. For a more radical take on things, Doug Henwood's *Left Business Observer* (http://www.leftbusinessobserver.com) is invaluable. The Canadian website, The Socialist Project (http://www.socialistproject.ca/), is very useful. The best English-language magazine on radical political economy and much else is *Monthly Review*, published continuously, since 1949.

Notes

1. See http://www.contactomagazine.com/biznews/unemployment2006.htm.
2. All national employment data can be found on the Bureau of Labor Statistics website: http://www.bls.gov.
3. See http://norris.blogs.nytimes.com/2009/06/05/long-term-unemployment-rate-hits-record/?hp.
4. See http://www.nytimes.com/2009/01/12/nyregion/12benefits.html.
5. See http://www.nypost.com/seven/04052009/business/near_future_shock_700_000_to_lose_joble_162965.htm.
6. See http://www.reuters.com/article/domesticNews/idUSTRE5314B320090402.
7. See, for example, http://news.brynmawr.edu/?p=1846.
8. See http://www.nytimes.com/2009/04/09/health/09stress.html?_r=2&emc=eta1; http://www.nytimes.com/2009/04/13/us/13burglar.html?_r=1&hp.
9. You can watch this on youtube: http://www.YouTube.com/watch?v=txw4GvEFGWs.
10. See http://www.rgemonitor.com/us-monitor/255066/why_so_little_self-recrimination_among_economists.
11. See Michael D. Yates, *Naming the System: Inequality and Work in the Global Economy* (New York: Monthly Review Press, 2002), chap. 1, for reasons why mainstream economists have such a limited understanding of capitalism.
12. See ibid., chap. 5, for a more detailed treatment.
13. See Lawrence Mishel, Jared Bernstein, and Heidi Shierholz, *The State of Working America, 2008/2009* (Ithaca, NY: Cornell University Press, 2009), chap. 3.
14. Much of the material in this chapter is based upon the classic account of stagnation: Paul A. Baran and Paul M. Sweezy, *Monopoly Capital* (New York: Monthly Review Press, 1968).
15. Calculated from Bureau of Economic Analysis table, "Current-Dollar and Real Gross Domestic Product," http://www.bea.gov/national/xls/gdplev.xls.
16. Federal Reserve, "Industrial Production and Capacity Utilization" table and chart, http://www.federalreserve.gov:80/releases/g17/Current/table0.htm; and http://www.federalreserve.gov:80/releases/g17/Current/ipg1.gif.
17. Data from the *Wall Street Journal*, April 4, 2009.
18. Calculated from Council of Economic Advisors, *2006 Economic Report of the President* (Washington DC: Government Printing Office, 2006), table B–91.

19. For more details on neoliberalism., see Yates, *Naming the System,* chap. 4.
20. For data on union membership, see the Bureau of Labor Statistics website (http://www.bls.gov). For the impact of unions on wages and benefits, see Michael D. Yates, *Why Unions Matter,* 2nd rev. ed. (New York: Monthly Review Press, 2009).
21. Data on wages and the distributions of income and wealth can be found in Mishel, Bernstein, and Shierholz, *The State of Working America, 2008/2009*, chaps. 2, 3, and 5.
22. On lean production and its impact on productivity and employment, see Kim Moody, *Labor in Trouble and Transition* (New York: Verso, 2007).
23. Bill Moyers, "Which America Will We Be Now?" *The Nation*, November 19, 2001.
24. On the financial explosion and a full development of the stagnation hypothesis applied to the "Great Recession," see John Bellamy Foster and Fred Magdoff, *The Great Financial Crisis: Causes and Consequences* (New York: Monthly Review Press, 2009). Most of the data in the remainder of this book are taken from this book.
25. See http://en.wikipedia.org/wiki/Economy_of_New_York_City.
26. Jill Drew, "Frenzy," *Washington Post,* December 16, 2008.
27. *Wall Street Journal*, March 3, 2006.
28. See http://www.nyse.com.
29. See http://www.bicusa.org/en/Article.11053.aspx.
30. Read the transcript of the Moyers-Black interview at http://www.pbs.org/moyers/journal/04032009/transcript1.html.
31. See http://www.nytimes.com/2008/12/07/business/07rating.html.
32. Calculated from tables L.1 and L.2 from the *Flow of Funds Accounts of the United States* (Federal Reserve); and table B-78 from the 2008 *Economic Report of the President.*
33. "Changes in Household Wealth in the 1980s and 1990s in the U.S.," table in *International Perspectives on Household Wealth,* ed. Edward N. Wolff (Northampton, MA: Edward Elgar Publishing, 2006).
34. Harry Magdoff and Paul M. Sweezy, *The Irreversible Crisis* (New York: Monthly Review Press, 1988), 76.
35. See http://en.wikipedia.org/wiki/Image:Shiller_IE2_Fig_2-1.png.
36. Moyers-Black interview.
37. Simon Johnson, "The Quiet Coup," *The Atlantic Monthly*, May 2009.
38. A useful timeline of economic policy enacted to combat the economic crisis has been compiled by the St. Louis Federal Reserve Bank; available at http://timeline.stlouisfed.org/.
39. Damian Palettal, David Enrich, and Deborah Solomon, "U.S. Rescue Aid Entrenches Itself," *Wall Street Journal,* May 29, 2009.
40. Katherine Boo, "Letter From Mumbai: Opening Night," *The New Yorker,* February 23, 2009, 22.

Index